Practical Knowledge and Information Management

T0322975

Practical Knowledge and Information Management

Katharine Schopflin and Matt Walsh

© Katharine Schopflin and Matt Walsh 2019

Published by Facet Publishing
7 Ridgmount Street, London WC1E 7AE
www.facetpublishing.co.uk

Facet Publishing is wholly owned by CILIP: the Library and Information Association.

Katharine Schopflin and Matt Walsh have asserted their right under the Copyright, Designs and Patents Act 1988 to be identified as authors of this work.

British Library Cataloguing in Publication Data
A catalogue record for this book is available from the British Library.

ISBN 978-1-78330-335-9 (paperback)
ISBN 978-1-78330-336-6 (hardback)
ISBN 978-1-78330-337-3 (e-book)

First published 2019

Text printed on FSC accredited material.

Typeset from author's files in 11/14 Elegant Garamond and Myriad Pro by Flagholme Publishing Services
Printed and made in Great Britain by CPI Group (UK) Ltd, Croydon, CR0 4YY.

Contents

Case studies and sidebars   vii

1   **Introduction to knowledge and information management**   **1**

Definition   2
The history of knowledge management   3
The history of information management   5
How knowledge and information management works   6
Further reading   9

2   **Introducing knowledge and information management**   **11**
    to organizations

Organizational culture and knowledge and information   11
management
Who needs knowledge management?   15
Introducing knowledge and information management   17
Making the case for knowledge and information management   21
Further reading   24

3   **Information management and governance**   **25**

Information and data repositories   28
Key points of advice for good information management   41
Governance and policies   41
Recommended approaches   51
Further reading   52

4   Communities and knowledge-sharing   **53**

Communication in the workplace   56
Supporting successful communities   68
Recommended approaches   72
Further reading   73

5   Making knowledge explicit: knowledge bases,   **75**
know-how and wikis

Knowledge organizing systems   78
Types of knowledge storage   82
Recommended approaches   90
Further reading   90

6   Capturing knowledge legacy: passing on staff   **91**
knowledge

Storytelling and 'show and tell'   93
Recommended approaches   95
After-action reviews and lessons learned   95
Knowledge capture from departing staff   100
Recommended approaches   106
Further reading   107

Afterword: the future of knowledge and information   **108**
management

References   **113**

Index   **117**

Case studies and sidebars

Chapter 2: Introducing knowledge and information management to organizations   **11**
Case study 2.1: Making KIM noticed   18
Case study 2.2: How not to introduce KIM   22

Chapter 3: Information management and governance   **25**
Case study 3.1: Core organizational data   31
Case study 3.2: The legacy of email   36
Sidebar: Six alternatives to email   37
Sidebar: A word about controls   40

Chapter 4: Communities and knowledge-sharing   **53**
Case study 4.1: Managing your online communities   62
Case study 4.2: Building a champions network   67
Sidebar: What to consider when managing online communities   72

Chapter 5: Making knowledge explicit: knowledge bases, know-how and wikis   **75**
Case study 5.1: Using your users' language   79
Sidebar: Types of taxonomies in knowledge and information management   81
Case study 5.2: Managing legal know-how   89

Chapter 6: Capturing knowledge legacy: passing on staff   **91**
knowledge
Case study 6.1: Learning from failure   97
Case study 6.2: The Capstone approach   104

Chapter 1

Introduction to knowledge and information management

While the special talent of the information professional will always be to connect users to the information or items they require, proactively or reactively, the actual work they carry out has changed considerably since the 1990s. Rather than being gatekeepers, they are now more likely to be advisers, interpreters, designers and trainers. In the library world 'librarian' is rare in job titles, particularly (but not exclusively) in the corporate or special library sector. Information professionals are increasingly involved with managing internal information in addition to connecting users to published resources. Meanwhile, records managers have moved from being the end-repository for corporate knowledge, instead frequently working with their colleagues to help them manage their own information from the moment it is created.

This book aims to provide a practical guide to knowledge and information management (KIM) for those working in organizations. It aims to complement the large body of management literature on the subject, and provide advice and best practice on the KIM work information professionals are required to do. As part of this, the authors have consulted professionals and reflected on their own experiences within the field. The book also aims to demonstrate new approaches to KIM and consider how developments may change its practice in the future.

Knowledge management (KM) emerged as a business practice in the 1980s. It has never been a practice exclusive to the information profession. Its purpose has been to enable organizations to do whatever they do as best they can, by facilitating the organization and sharing of tacit and expressed knowledge. It is most often associated with corporate bodies. However, the authors believe it applies in any organization. A recent article (Daland, 2016) considered the benefits of KM to academic libraries, where providing access to published materials has traditionally been the central role of its service. Townley's 2001 article 'Knowledge Management and Academic Libraries' concluded that approaches from KM would benefit academic libraries. And the last part of Seely Brown and Duguid's *The Social Life of Information* (2002) showed presciently how academic learning is affected as much by institutional experience as by learning materials themselves. Perhaps because of their multiple missions and varied users, public libraries have found KIM less relevant. Individual examples can be found in a session from the 2012 International Federation of Library Associations Conference (IFLA, 2012) and a 2002 article by Teng and Hawamdeh, which considered KM to be part of a national organizing strategy for library provision. In all these cases, librarians are urged to think beyond the library's role as a keeper of collections, and to consider instead how knowledge owned by and useful to its communities can be better disseminated.

While most of our case studies come from the corporate sector, we hope we will demonstrate the value of KIM in any setting. Put simply, what organization does not benefit from knowing how best to find and use its internal expertise and information? The succeeding chapters will look at different types of KIM challenges and practice. This chapter will set out a definition and history, and identify the benefits and challenges.

Definition

This book is about KIM but it is common to make distinctions between KM and information management (IM). The former is considered to be any mechanism that enables the use of tacit knowledge: knowledge held inside people's heads. The latter concerns the organization, dissemination and storage of recorded knowledge. While these distinctions are a useful starting point, in reality the distinction is blurred. Some believe that it is impossible to capture tacit knowledge, that as soon as a piece of knowledge is articulated, it is in some way expressed, and has thus 'become' information (Wilson, 2002, is an example). By that definition, managing knowledge is difficult, but not impossible. Organizations can facilitate the opportunities for knowledge to be shared and expressed, but as soon as the latter happens, it is information which is managed.

Another common means of representing the distinction is to consider the two on this continuum: data – information – knowledge – wisdom (some writers insert 'competency' between knowledge and wisdom). One can move along the continuum from data (points of information without meaning beyond themselves), to information (where data is interpreted and thus provide new meaning) to knowledge (where the context of the information is understood and can be internalised) to wisdom (where the long-term acquisition of knowledge enables informed decisions, insight and strategy). Of course each of these terms is open to interpretation. The anthropologist Geoffrey Bateson (1972, 336) suggested that an 'elementary unit of information' is 'a difference that makes a difference', suggesting there is a relationship between the introduction of a new item and a change in the person who acquires it. The point that the 'difference' is made could be between 'data' and 'information' or between 'information' and 'knowledge'. For others, the definition of 'knowledge' is closer to the one given here for 'wisdom', that it is information internalised and made able to inform future decisions. There is a clear distinction between atomised information with no context and information that can be used and acted on. At which point in the continuum the transformation takes place is open to interpretation.

In the workplace, KIM takes a variety of forms, which we will cover later in the book. A knowledge and information manager might be involved in policy-making, compliance, training, communications, storage, technology custodianship, business process engineering, office design and all manner of facilitation of finding and organizing digital objects. The following definition, while vague, covers most of them:

> Knowledge and information management is a range of systematic approaches taken to enable organizations to achieve success through making the best use of the knowledge and expertise available to them.

The following chapters outline many of these approaches, describe factors in their success and failure, and demonstrate how they can best be achieved.

The history of knowledge management

KM theory, although it did not yet have this name (its activities can be found under such terms as 'business process re-engineering' and 'intellectual capital'), emerged in the 1970s from a range of academic disciplines, including philosophy, management theory, information technology, economics and sociology, largely in the USA. A combination of the decline of manufacturing industries and rising labour costs encouraged theorists to consider how organizations could work differently, in a world where their unique selling point could not simply be the ability to produce large numbers of goods as cheaply as possible. Theorists from Stanford and MIT suggested that the true value of organizations in long-established industrial countries was actually in their intellectual capital. This encompassed such things as the knowledge built up over decades and stored in the heads of current staff, in procedures and practices passed from employee to employee and in corporate documents, manuals and records of decisions. Looking at corporate structure, motivation to work and the flow of knowledge in organizations, they suggested that workforces could achieve more if knowledge were shared more across organizational divisions.

One approach taken by early adopters of these theories was to reorganize their businesses on vertical lines. Traditionally, organizations separated their 'thinking' and 'doing' areas and also those facing internal and externally. This meant that research and development, production and marketing and sales not only did not communicate with each other, but also developed their own tacit or explicit knowledge bases, which were not shared across the organization. Knowledge taken for granted by those who sold products was not communicated back to those who developed and made them. A corporate structure based on subject-specific areas of expertise across all types of work could achieve efficiencies, innovation and engender greater profits. Sharing knowledge across functional areas engendered a better understanding of customers and extracted more value out of an increasingly expensive workforce. While property, inventory, equipment and other physical assets might lose value over time, the corporate knowledge base only became more valuable. A structure which supported its dissemination could only increase organizations' competitive advantage.

During the 1980s and 1990s KM moved into the mainstream, as conferences, publications, academic disciplines and workplace roles emerged. Wilson (2002) observes that 'knowledge management' as a term first appeared in the literature cited in the citation indexing service Web of Science in 1986 and increased greatly in popularity after 1997. Management consultancies, in particular McKinsey & Co, were highly influential in these years in advising KM approaches to their clients. This helped to popularise KM concepts with senior managers. During this period, many developments in KM were based around technology (Wilson noted that published research from around the turn of the century overwhelmingly concerned information systems). Much organizational change and expenditure in 'adopting KM' involved the purchase and implementation of expensive KM systems. Ironically, a discipline which had evolved out of the study of people became one where technology was considered the solution to the lack of knowledge-sharing and capture. By the 21st century, KM consultancy and staff roles (usually based in IT departments) were common in large organizations. KM became a growth area for recruitment, stretching beyond IT implementation and embracing training, internal communications and all types of change processes. To some extent this has decreased as the second decade has progressed. Both the authors of this book have seen KM departments established and closed during this time. However, organizations continue to appreciate the importance of KM practice and to hire people to facilitate it.

The history of information management

For as long as there has been recorded information there have been efforts to ensure that it can be found again and referred to. The world of administration has always relied on shared systems to ensure multiple parties understand the what, how and who of agreements, expenditure, production, life and death. Developments such as alphabetic writing, paper, index cards, loose-leafs, classification systems and mechanical and electronic computing have all been used to facilitate IM. As the quantity of recorded information has increased, so have concerns about our ability to control and keep track of its contents. Systems for the organization of information have been proposed throughout the centuries, on a personal level, within particular institutions and, as the discipline of archives was developed, at a national scale.

Like KM, the modern discipline of IM emerged from management concerns about efficiency, albeit with a recognition that the traditional skills of librarians and archivists were part of the solution. A report by the Hawley Committee (1995) commissioned from consulting firm KPMG expressed senior executives' concerns that they had lost control over the information in their organizations. They had also become increasingly aware that, in a service rather than a manufacturing economy, well-managed information was essential to maintain competitive edge. There was a sense in these organizations that information technology would be the solution to this problem. IM systems, concerned more with the benefits of free-text search than with proactive organization, were the focus for organizations from the 1990s onwards.

However, managers in organizations did not anticipate the fundamental change to the workplace brought by modern desktop software. Until the 1990s, electronic records in most organizations were confined to a few, highly controlled systems. While some staff had word processors, the bulk of unstructured organizational records were managed by teams of secretaries, typists and filing clerks, following systems to ensure that information could be found when needed and was kept for as long as necessary. Over time this changed so that everyone managed their own correspondence and documents in electronic spaces.

Organizations started to create huge bodies of recorded information, held in documents, spreadsheets, presentations, media files, e-mail and increasingly disparate social media applications. Within them useful, important or vital records often became hidden among what records managers term 'ROT' – the redundant, outdated and trivial. The modern discipline of IM is essentially different tactics to deal with this problem.

However, the prominence of IM roles in the 21st century possibly has less to do with a recognition of this crisis than with changes in information legislation. Freedom of information legislation was first introduced in the USA in 1966, in Australia in 1982 and across Europe in the 1990s. The requirement to respond to requests for public information makes it essential for public bodies to know where their information is and desirable to make it public where they can. The increasing challenge of the task in the face of uncontrolled electronic repositories provided a boost to the records management profession in the 1990s and many new roles were created. Meanwhile data protection legislation was introduced in the UK and Australia in the 1980s (and amended in subsequent years) in response to concerns about electronic data. To comply, organizations needed to ensure they only keep as much personal information as necessary and only for as long as it is needed. Most jurisdictions also offer individuals the right to know what data is held about them and obtain copies of it.

Such legislation has made it essential that information is managed. For many, powerful search and cheap electronic storage space was considered the solution to the crisis of unmanaged information, but this remains insufficient to meet legal requirements to know in advance where information is and to delete it when no longer needed. While information managers have always argued that it is an organization's interest to know where their important information is, compliance has provided an impetus for proactive IM and a need for expert staff to carry it out. In 2018, the General Data Protection Regulation (GDPR) was adopted in the European Economic Area, with a far greater requirement for organizations to demonstrate that their business practices met the principles of good data handling. This alone has provided a boost to the status and number of corporate information managers.

How knowledge and information management works

The two previous sections outlined how the KIM profession emerged out of a desire to use fully the knowledge and expertise of staff on one hand, and to keep control over recorded information on the other. How they combine varies hugely depending on the organization.

In her book *Information Strategy in Practice*, Elizabeth Orna (2004, 9) outlined a synthesised approach to KIM, suggesting that it should cover how to:

* identify organizational knowledge needs
* identify the knowledge in employees' heads
* maintain and safeguard this knowledge
* transform knowledge into information
* advise on rights and obligations
* promote knowledge exchange
* provide systems and technical support
* provide organizational learning.

There are many different approaches to achieving success in these areas, including by looking at technical solutions, organizational design and developing workforce 'intellectual capital' (Wiig, 1997). Wiig identifies three main areas of emphasis in KIM:

* top-down approaches – looking at the organization as a whole, through knowledge audits, process flows and organizational design
* creating knowledge infrastructure, such as ontologies, inventories or structured repositories
* renewing, organizing and transferring knowledge by populating knowledge bases, and encouraging collaboration, learning and training.

This makes for a variety of roles. Some of the above can be achieved through well-defined roles in audit, information security, developing knowledge repositories, information compliance, system development, support and training. Other aspects could be achieved in high-level analytical and policy work, identifying the information needs of the organization and suggesting solutions. KIM workers may be carrying out highly structured process-driven work such as classification, taxonomy development or data auditing. Or they could be in hard-to-define roles aimed at facilitating knowledge-sharing, running communities of practice, making technology more effective and encouraging learning opportunities. More detail on what these roles entail will be covered in later chapters.

Where KIM sits within the organization can affect the nature of roles and activities. Those delivering KM functions in IT departments are naturally focused on software solutions. Where KIM teams have grown from an existing information service, perhaps replacing a physical library, the team tend to focus on information artefacts such as knowledge bases and team sites. KM teams that sit within human resources may be more concerned with internal social media and training and perhaps compliance. Meanwhile, Knowledge and Information Managers concerned with policy and compliance can often sit at the very top of organizations, with the ear of the most senior staff, but then struggle to see their work translated into behaviour.

The challenges of organizational KIM should not be underestimated. Initiatives based on management theories can seem irrelevant to the day-to-day work of busy staff, who certainly do not want their practices interfered with by a non-expert. Work cultures which reward individual effort (through bonuses or, in creative workplaces, with commissions and publications) effectively punish their staff for sharing knowledge. Depending on the organizational culture, staff can be too afraid to share, too concerned with security or simply want to avoid being seen 'not working'. Even non-traditional workplaces experience cultures of suspicion that those who have time to participate in organizational knowledge projects must be under-employed elsewhere. And if results do not appear quickly, which – if behavioural and cultural change is necessary – they certainly will not, managers can question the wisdom of employing KIM staff.

KIM also must engage with legacy technology and organizational structures. Organizations tend to run two or more lines of business systems, used by a large body of staff to fulfil core functions. Ideally, new workflows inspired by KIM approaches should be incorporated into these systems. If not, the KIM function has the challenge of drawing workers from the systems they use every day into other spaces. Similarly, simply reorganizing a workforce may not address hidden cultural allegiances. A newly reorganized workforce, or one brought in through takeover or merger, is likely to come with legacy systems and ways of working. Knowledge and information managers must engage with this and find ways of working across historical barriers.

If the above challenges did not exist, then there would be no need for KIM. More than ever before organizations need to know what they know – to know where to put their information, where to find it and who to ask. They need to know what they are allowed to do with their information (whether contractually or through legislation) and to feel safe making choices about deleting or keeping it. They need to know where to find previously recorded knowledge, so that they do not have to repeat work, and can learn from previous mistakes. And they need to encourage the exchange of diverse and creative ideas to ensure that whatever they do, they do it as well as they can.

The next chapter concentrates in detail on how KM works in organizations, how different cultures deal with KIM and approaches you might take when trying to improve KIM practice. It will suggest what to consider if you plan to introduce an initiative within an organization and how you make your case for it. Chapter 3 looks at traditional IM approaches, auditing and governance. Chapter 4 looks at people-based initiatives, forming communities of practice, sharing knowledge and using team sites. Chapter 5 examines methods of making knowledge explicit through knowledge bases, wikis and best practice manuals. Chapter 6 explores managing knowledge and information legacy, capturing the intellectual capital of a mobile workforce and taking lessons learned forward.

We cannot claim to be entirely comprehensive in KIM practice, but we hope this book will cover the majority of activities a KIM professional is likely to be involved in. And we cannot predict the future, but we hope we will give an idea of how we think it will evolve.

Further reading

Orna, E. (2004) *Information Strategy in Practice*, Gower.

Seely Brown, J. and Duguid, P. (2000) *The Social Life of Information*, Harvard Business School Press.

Wiig, K. M. (1997) Knowledge Management: an introduction and perspective, *Journal of Knowledge Management*, 1 (1), 6–14, https://doi.org/10.1108/13673279710800682.

Wilson, T. D. (2002) The Nonsense of Knowledge Management, *Information Research*, 8 (1), 144–54.

Wilson, T. D. (2005) The Nonsense of Knowledge Management Revisited. In Macevičūtė, E. and Wilson, T. (eds), *Introducing Information Management: an information research reader*, Facet Publishing, 151–64.

Chapter 2

Introducing knowledge and information management to organizations

This chapter will look at how to introduce KIM in organizations and how it works. We will examine how organizations are designed and how knowledge and information flows within them, what barriers can appear and how a knowledge and information manager can tackle them. We will look at the challenges of introducing KIM, how different types of organizations respond to KIM initiatives and how you can work with organizational culture to achieve your aims. We will consider a range of approaches, from large-scale, top-down programmes to small-problem-solving initiatives and strategies for success in different contexts.

Organizational culture and knowledge and information management

Any area of work that uses learning, skills and know-how can benefit from KIM. In her book *The Outrun* (Liptrot, 2016), Amy Liptrot describes how her parents developed an operative sheep farm in Orkney. Her mother was brought up on a farm, so carried with her considerable internalised knowledge. Her father attended agricultural college and obtained formal skills. Once they had started their sheep farm, the family kept in touch with other members of the community and shared with them new techniques, ideas and problem-solving approaches. But there were specifics to the particular piece of land they were farming. Over a decade, they tried out different approaches until they found a set of practices which worked for their location. Finally, once established, the sheep themselves learned the best means of adapting to the land, habits which, as Liptrot described it, became inbred over generations. In this example, a combination of ingrained knowledge, acquired skills, knowledge-sharing, legacy learning and adaptation produced an organization which worked for its specific circumstances. Other factors which contributed were buying new technology and hiring staff with particular skills. KIM works in similar ways in organizations. The challenge for the KIM professional is to find the best ways of optimising all types of knowledge for organizational circumstances.

There is no ideal culture for KIM. The authors have worked in a range of organizational cultures, from the very liberal to the very conservative, and there are barriers to adoption in both areas. Liberal organizations with a relaxed working lifestyle and a mature approach to communication may embrace internal social media and be great informal knowledge-sharers. But they are likely to chafe at formal initiatives, or anything designed to make them manage their expressed knowledge according to rules. More conservative organizations may welcome structure and respond well to policies advising them how to manage their documents, but may be nervous of any informal approach to knowledge-sharing. And absolutely no organization will share knowledge and expertise if staff are rewarded for keeping it to themselves.

This speaks to a paradox in KIM. Although both KM and IM aim to enable intellectual capital of an organization to be found and used in the best way possible, typical methods for KM at its softest tend to centre around creating opportunities for knowledge exchange, whereas those for IM tend to be around policies and guidance for where and how information should be stored. One speaks to order and structure, the other to creativity and opportunity. As a result organizations that are good at one are often less good at the other.

Management theorists have much to say about organizational culture. In his influential book *Understanding Organizations*, Charles Handy identified four different types of organization, differing on where the source of power and influence lay. These were the entrepreneur-led 'power culture', the 'role culture' led by an oligarchy of bureaucrats, the meritocratic, expert-led 'task culture' and the individualistic 'person culture' (1976, 181–91). Handy himself admits that these categories are 'impressionistic and imprecise' but they are a useful way of thinking about what motivates people to perform well and what can form barriers in trying to influence employee behaviour. Davenport and Prusak (1998) outline organizational 'markets' for knowledge, in which the 'buyers', 'sellers' and 'brokers' of knowledge are motivated by a range of forces to acquire or share their expertise (1998, 27–36). This speaks to the imbalance of knowledge and information among different types of worker in many organizations, often reflecting deeply ingrained hierarchies. In general, most conclude that employees share knowledge and information when motivated to do so by financial reward, job satisfaction or personal identification with company success, and when it is made easy for them to do so by internal systems. Organizational cultures can therefore work both for and against the sharing of knowledge.

Wenger (1998, 244–5) identifies three ways through which organizations embed particular kinds of culture:

- *roles, qualifications and the distribution of authority*, which define who is important in the organization, how you can progress, and what you will be rewarded and punished for
- *charters, targets and systems of measurements*, the most powerful means of dictating what staff do from day to day; most staff will not do anything that prevents them from achieving the things on which they are measured
- *procedures, contracts, rules, processes and policies*, the weakest method; Wenger suggests that staff decide 'when to comply with them and when to ignore them'.

But these are not the only means by which organizational culture displays itself, and it can be useful when you introduce KIM to consider many different aspects of working life. Questions you might think about are:

- What hours do people work? How much freedom do they have to change this?
- How do people talk to each other? How much informal language is used?
- What are the mechanisms for communication? Could anyone talk to anyone – and if so, how? Would it be unusual for a low-paid worker to speak out at a staff conference? Do people feel happy leaving messages on internal communications channels?
- How locked-down are IT systems? Do people share calendars? Network drives? Works in progress?
- Who are the most highly paid in the organization and who else do they talk to internally?
- What is the layout of the office and how do people work in it? If it is open plan, do many staff use headphones? Do people genuinely hot-desk?
- How is financial reward and promotion managed? (These are not always the same thing.)
- What other benefits are on offer? Is there a staff canteen or trolley? Is tea and coffee provided?

Variations in the practicalities of working life such as those addressed in the questions above are just some of the ways in which an organization displays its identity in the behaviours of its employees. And, contrary to the idea that we can judge the workers of the future by looking at the children of today, such cultures are easily absorbed by new staff. In fact, these people are more likely to obey the unwritten rules in an attempt to fit in (unless of course they find them unbearable and intend to leave) than more established staff who may feel they have more freedom to be themselves.

Typically, most organizations have a group of workers who are considered the most valuable and essential to what it is that they do. In a policy or advisory organization (and in most parts of central government) these are most likely to be professional expert advisers, who carry out analysis, provide advice and draft documents. They are likely to have a strong peer identification with each other and are motivated to share knowledge, although physical isolation may prevent regular interaction. However, they are often the least likely in the organization to have regular contact with the users of the product or service. This is usually delivered by frontline staff such as call-centre workers, often the lowest-paid and least valued in the organization (although users are increasingly encouraged to access information about the service themselves). It is considered a poor use of resource to put highly paid experts into transactional work, so their knowledge often fails to reach frontline workers. John Seddon ably demonstrates the problems this can cause in *The Whitehall Effect* (2014), where he discusses how the separation of 'front' and 'back office' leads to 'demand generation' – more work needed on transactions that cannot be solved simply. It is the role of the knowledge and information manager to make sure that expertise can reach all parts of organizations, which may involve confronting hierarchies and challenging the most important people within it.

In a technology organization, the most valued members of staff are usually either software engineers or sales representatives. Such organizations can be highly liberal in their cultural norms, provided the quality and rate of work produced is adequate. Software engineers are often allowed freedom of working hours and practices, and can be exempt from corporate training and initiatives. In an organization where sales staff are valued as the people who pay everybody else's salaries, they may have similar freedom of behaviour. The result can be work carried out in a vacuum, where each side fails to connect and cannot be compelled to use corporate repositories or learning platforms. Ideally, this would be mitigated through a linking team, such as customer support or business development, or in a workplace employing agile methodologies, a product manager. However, the former requires mutual respect and value, which may not be present in the company hierarchy, and the latter puts a strong level of responsibility on a single role. The result can be sales staff selling without accurately representing the product and technologists working without a clear understanding of changing customer needs.

These are just two examples of how different organizational culture may prevent knowledge and information from flowing within organizations. Size, global footprint, attitude to technology, and age also influence how knowledge and information are treated. This indicates that there is no one-size-fits-all approach to introducing a knowledge initiative. You will need to adjust your strategy to meet the culture, not the other way around. Moreover, many organizations support multiple sub-cultures, which for historic or practical reasons are not challenged by organizational norms. Even within an organization different approaches may be necessary to solve the problems of KIM.

Who needs knowledge management?

As the list above indicates, there are other aspects to organizational culture than hierarchy which may create barriers and 'opportunities'. Here are some examples of 'oppportunities' to improve organizations with KIM.

Procurement

Heavily controlled and centralised purchasing systems which everyone must use have for many years been seen as a means of controlling both financial decisions and avoiding other risks (for example, that a supplier may go bust or be involved in a public scandal). This is an opportunity to ensure that corporate knowledge is saved in a single system. However cheap cloud-based applications are increasingly affordable to any middle manager with budgetary authority. Even office-based products such as spreadsheets may be used as a solution if a company-wide system does not suit a particular team, meaning both corporate knowledge and potential information repositories are dispersed and uncontrolled. This is an example of how an attempt at central control can fail if staff do not feel compelled to obey the rules. In some organizations, micro-services are the norm. In these organizations, the advantage of using a system which is the best at what it does for the immediate task outweighs the fact that subsequently corporate knowledge may be scattered across many different applications.

Human resources

The need to get paid, book leave and claim work-related benefits is something staff in all organizations have in common. It is therefore an essential, but often neglected area, to improve productivity. Does the administrative burden lie with employees, their managers or with a central team? And do the responsibilities of each match their rights over the systems? As the one area that employees are heavily motivated to maintain accurately, self-service can often seem like a means of saving on support staff, but many self-service systems merely transfer the transactional burden onto staff whose main job is elsewhere. This is a good opportunity to demonstrate how KIM can improve productivity. Systems which lead staff and managers through a transaction gathering exactly the information needed will reduce the time spent away from daily work. Organizations with a large central human resources operation may benefit from advice about how to manage, gather and maintain staff data.

Diversity

Although equal opportunities legislation exists in many countries, and most organizations state that they aim to have a diverse workforce, most support certain types of voice more than others. In purely commercial terms, this means that certain types of culture are replicated and opportunities for innovation and new ideas missed. Offering an online discussion forum will not help unempowered staff who may fear repercussions unless the culture itself supports hearing diverse voices. In some cases, it may simply be impractical for staff to contribute to online systems if they work in a front office situation, or their time is heavily measured. It is a challenge for KIM to be able to offer opportunities for voices throughout the organization that fit in with the way these staff are compelled to work. However, it is also an opportunity to hold organizations to account for their statements on staff diversity.

Technical capability

Organizations with a large number of technically aware staff may seem to be better candidates for adopting new ways of working, and using collaborative knowledge systems. However, corporate systems often use compromise technologies, chosen because they enable a number of tasks to be performed adequately, rather than any single one well. This is likely to frustrate and alienate staff who are familiar with better products and have the technical ability to find alternatives for themselves. This is a challenge for KIM as these staff may opt out of collaborative corporate products. Conversely, it should not be considered a drawback when staff are less technically able, but a challenge to ensure that they are presented with systems they can easily learn to use. The latter may require more support to build their confidence in using them but, if this is offered, may be better candidates for adoption.

Having considered some of the potential issues a knowledge and information manager may face when starting their work, the next section looks at how KIM initiatives are typically brought into organizations.

Introducing knowledge and information management

In the early part of the 21st century, KIM typically entered an organization by being adopted at the very highest level in an organization. Whether as a result of consultancy advice or through attending conferences or management training, an influential member of senior staff would learn about KIM techniques and recognise the advantages they could bring to their organization. After all, what could be more attractive than an approach which uses an organization's existing assets? Surely this is a supremely cost-effective means of creating value with minimal effort? Ensuing actions might be appointing a new manager, team or role, developing a suite of policies and procedures, purchasing business-wide technology and introducing widely publicised corporate initiatives. In many cases these executives were attempting to tackle acknowledged organizational problems. Many led from the front by adopting new ways of working themselves. Such 'knowledge programmes' were common in the first decade of the 21st century.

It could be argued that this was the worst possible way to introduce KIM. In her paper 'Success in Knowledge Management', Schopflin (2015) argued that KIM programmes involve the newest staff in the organization having to challenge well-established cultures and influential employees. KIM is considered to be something separate from, additional to and even challenging to core organizational work. In such cases the senior originator of the knowledge programme may themselves be reluctant to challenge entrenched behaviour of these important staff. And yet, expectations about the level of change achieved may be high, an actual revolution in knowledge-sharing behaviours being expected. If this is not achieved, the knowledge programme may be considered a failure and the KIM roles be closed, as a poor return on investment.

Corporate technology platforms were often purchased or configured as part of such programmes, perhaps using a corporate-wide taxonomy developed by a KIM professional. The idea behind developing this technology was to ensure a

Case study 2.1: Making KIM noticed

Organization B is an old, family-run organization, which has grown by buying other businesses (specifically, the market leaders at what they did in each new country they expanded into). This created a dispersed culture supporting autonomy in each territory, albeit aligned to a strong mission statement. Individual divisions were allowed to grow organically and staff could adopt their own approaches, as long as they were successful and consistent with the organization's ethos and approach.

However, it was recognised that this had created a huge body of undocumented knowledge across the different divisions from which the business as a whole could benefit. In response to this, a new role, global head of KM, was created. The appointee was an experienced practitioner from within the business, new to KM, but who understood the business well, and had good relationships in most areas.

As a starting point, the new head articulated a vision of how KM could work over time, starting with an agreed definition of terms, moving onto organizing and structuring knowledge and then moving onto creating the circumstances for sharing. Although publicised as a corporate-wide initiative, developing the whole organization as a knowledge-sharing body, it was expected that it would take time before KM was widely adopted.

Having announced the knowledge programme, it was felt important to implement a KIM product quickly, to produce something tangible to win the organization's trust. An online knowledge-base, designed to encapsulate the top level of shared corporate knowledge, was developed and quickly launched. The product was not initially interactive but instead aimed to define commonly-used terms and concepts, based on prior consultation from within the business. The backing of the global head of KIM was essential in enabling the compilers to access knowledge from around the business and to overcome technical barriers to its deployment. Although it needed subsequent refining, it gained high awareness and notable use within the business, paving the way for future initiatives.

The concept of a corporate encyclopedia was, in the age of the wiki, backward-looking, but it suited the culture of the organization. While its uses were limited, it gained a high degree of recognition quickly. KIM staff had demonstrated that a highly publicised programme could achieve an outcome. Moreover, the relationships built during the process of building it were essential in identifying the next steps in KIM.

In this example, the launch of a KIM programme was followed by the achievement of a KIM initiative in a short period of time. They achieved success by aiming for a solid outcome, actionable largely by the KIM team themselves. While the outcome itself was modest in KIM terms, senior management recognised that it was a starting point on a longer journey towards greater knowledge-sharing. Moreover, as the idea originated with a senior, long-serving member of staff in a dedicated KIM role, impediments to completing the project were minimised. It therefore became a good starting point for future achievements and helped to establish the reputation of the team.

single repository for corporate knowledge and expertise. But compelling staff to use such technology is difficult, particularly if is not the main platform on which they carry out their job. KIM systems often develop bad reputations and are considered expensive white elephants, or heavily resented. Encouraging staff to use them can be a challenge. For example, performance measures can make engagement with KIM artificial, if staff only engage with systems because their bonuses depend on a certain number of interactions. And alternatives to centralised systems are increasingly available. It may be more productive to consider how knowledge could be shared from within the systems staff are already using. In the past restrictive licensing and poor reporting tools meant that systems used by a small group would be walled gardens of knowledge and information not available to the rest of the organization. More relaxed licensing regimes can help and with better reporting even if only one team can input data, the whole organization should be able to view system outputs.

Instead of a heavily promoted, top-down knowledge programme, a better approach is to consider what problems need solving in your organization and how KIM can help. This is not to say that senior buy-in is not important. In fact, it may be essential (although the level of seniority depends on what you are trying to achieve). But good KIM practice can more easily be achieved by stealth than by coercion.

Here are the authors' top recommendations.

▪ Don't try a single approach for a whole organization

As mentioned above, different parts of an organization may have different cultures and certainly will have different problems. Address the diversity of your organization by considering the types of solutions that work for individual areas or groups of users. These groups do not have to be existing business units. It is still possible to fulfil the aim of KIM – to enable organizations to share knowledge across organizational boundaries – without attempting to make everyone do the same thing.

▪ Use existing communities and aim to help them

In their book *The Social Life of Information*, Seely Brown and Duguid discussed research carried out by the anthropologist Julian Orr into photocopier repair workers whose learning and development benefited most not from formal training, but from an informal breakfast where they shared problems (2000, 99–105). This is a community of practice which already existed and demonstrated excellent results from collaboration and knowledge transfer. The role of the knowledge and information manager is to identify existing communities and find out what they can do to support them, rather than force them to use a corporately devised solution. Don't dismiss a knowledge base created using sub-optimal technology and poor categorisation. Instead, offer to improve it. These users are your foot soldiers in introducing KIM to the rest of the organization. Improve the existing product then work with their creators to showcase those enhancements.

■ *Seek to solve problems that people actually recognise as problems*

The best method of introducing good KIM practice is to use it to solve something that is perceived as a problem. The solution might be with a tool, a business process, training or simply by putting the right people in touch. You may have better results if you do not brand your efforts with 'knowledge and information management'. For the users, the problem is one of whatever they do – research, sales, marketing, customer service – not KIM. But you can use your success in this area to show what KIM can achieve.

■ *Start small*

It can be tempting to launch into a high-profile project and, indeed, it may be what you have been employed to do. This is a dangerous approach, as any failure will be equally high profile. If possible, aim for something achievable and wait until you have a better understanding of the organization before you attempt serious change. You cannot achieve an organization-wide change without the buy-in of those who need to adopt it. You are more likely to achieve this buy-in if you have won their trust by solving smaller problems first.

■ *Consult users*

It is essential to have support from above when attempting to improve or change how people work. And you must have buy-in from middle managers if you are working with their teams. They may be anxious to keep control over their staff and their performance, which after all is the main thing on which they are measured. But do consult users. You may be surprised by the results. Your IT helpdesk staff may welcome the idea of a structured repository for their knowledge and information, even if their managers have assumed that they would not want to be hidebound by it. They also have the best knowledge of the frustrations and inefficiencies of existing processes and systems. In organizations where their voices are little heard, this may be an untapped source for innovation and improvement.

■ *Ensure policies can be put into practice*

Chapter 3 explores the problem of the policy as the artefact. This is not to say that policies are not useful. They are the building blocks on which guidance and practice are built. However, they should be short and realistic. Consider them as an aid to help people make decisions, rather than a series of rules which employees are supposed to abide. Your guidance and processes are the bridge between your policy and how people actually work. Make sure it is possible for it to reach both banks.

■ *Approach internal services teams*

Human resources, IT and finance are functions which exist in most sizeable organizations (unless outsourced). Their systems and products are used by employees in every area and yet, because they are not income centres, they are often neglected when system and process improvement is considered. An improved intranet or better IT know-how can reap obvious efficiencies very quickly. And these areas may welcome help and advice where more high-profile departments would resent it.

■ Engage with learning and development

It is important to establish that KIM complements, rather than supplants organizational training initiatives. A good learning and development team will listen to what you would like to achieve and consider the kind of development offer which could help. Staff can help incorporate good KIM practice into their courses, helping to demonstrate that KIM is carried out by everyone in the organization, not just KIM professionals.

■ Learn what has happened before

What have been the organization's biggest successes and failures of the previous years? If they have had a previous failed KIM initiative, be prepared to meet resistance. Show that you understand what went wrong in the past and how you want to do things differently this time. And build on any recent successes – if there is anything you can replicate from them, you may achieve similar results.

Making the case for knowledge and information management

How you make the case for KIM depends very much on what you wish to achieve and your position within the organization. Here are some possible scenarios.

I have been appointed as a knowledge manager to solve the organization's KIM problems

You have a hard task ahead of you. It shouldn't be necessary, but the first thing you need to do is agree some realistic expectations of achievement. It is too common for the appointment of KIM roles to be considered the solution to widespread corporate problems. As mentioned above, a new middle-ranking member of staff is unlikely to be able to achieve this, although they can be the instrument in solving other problems. You need support and some achievable outcomes in reasonable timeframes. And if your manager does not have the influence to challenge the behaviour of other staff, they cannot expect you to.

You have the advantage that for your role to have been created, you have the buy-in of someone at a reasonably high level. You need to assess how far this gives you a mandate within your organization. Once this is established, you can then

Case study 2.2: How not to introduce KIM

Organization A is a successful research and information function in a long-established organization with well-entrenched traditions and hierarchies. A team internal to the department had been established for a range of IM tasks, but staff were considered functionaries, rather than having any influence over how research was carried out or services delivered. They found it difficult to challenge entrenched behaviours and were themselves reluctant to undertake new initiatives.

A senior role was created as manager of the team and with the specific task of writing an organizational knowledge and information strategy and introducing it to the business. The role was deliberately senior as the person holding it was expected to try and create influence within the organization.

Although the strategy was signed off at senior level, attempts to persuade senior research staff to adopt it in their own behaviour encountered barriers. These expert staff, renowned for delivering an extremely high level of work in special circumstances, saw no reason to share their knowledge more widely or follow any new procedures. In most cases these employees were on the same grade or higher as the KIM role and felt empowered to dismiss any advice they were given.

Senior managers acknowledged that because of the special status of these expert staff they were unlikely ever to embrace new ways of working. They accepted that the investment in KM had not been successful and the team disappeared in a subsequent restructure.

Two key flaws in this approach made success very difficult to achieve. The first was that those who created and appointed the post never had any intention of challenging behaviours within the organization. They somehow believed that appointing somebody junior to them would achieve that. The second was the belief that writing and developing a strategy document would achieve the desired changes. The existence of the document, signed off at the highest level, could not compel staff to share and record their knowledge and expertise and their own managers had no appetite to make them.

start engaging with the business at all levels. Introduce yourself, listen to people's problems, shadow people and sit in on their team meetings (if they let you). Some people will be more open to meeting you than others. Ask their advice about how to engage with the rest of the business.

Identify one or two things that you can help resolve. Here you may need to go back to more senior management for the resources or influence necessary to achieve your aim. Pick something that will make users' life easier, even if improvements in productivity are not immediately obvious.

If it works, tell everyone else about it, at every level in the organization. And keep engaging with the users to get their feedback about how it could be improved.

I am experienced in the organization and want to improve things
You have a major advantage that you already have a role and a track record within the organization. But you need to make your case on the basis of tangible problems and their solutions. Ideally your KIM initiative should also address a corporate priority.

Identify a specific problem that you think that a KIM initiative could solve, and how you think it would change matters. Identify potential costs, including training, cultural change and loss of productivity while staff adjust. Identify a time frame for implementation and one for when you expect to see positive results, whatever they might be.

Work closely with the manager of staff most likely to be affected and gather credible evidence of what the initiative will achieve. Find examples of where it has worked with similar organizations. Then take the proposal higher. Emphasise how it will help both the organization as a whole and senior staff to achieve their objectives. And make sure your own behaviour is consistent with it (for example, if your initiative is to reduce the number of e-mails received within the organization, then adopt the measures you recommend to others).

You are in a good position to use your success to encourage better KIM practice and more initiatives across the organization.

I work with a specific group and would like to help them
Congratulations! You have the best likelihood of a successful outcome. You already have their support and buy-in, have a good understanding of the issues they face, and can consider the range of KIM techniques to help them do what they do better.

If your group is a low-profile or uninfluential group within the organization, you may have to come up with solutions that do not cost money, or which cause very little disruption outside this group. The disadvantage to this is that some of the best options may only be achievable with the financial or managerial support. The advantage is that you can bring in better ways of working under the radar, without having to win buy-in from reluctant or difficult-to-access managers.

However, if you can make incremental changes that demonstrate success in your area, you can highlight this, bring the spotlight onto the group you are working with and potentially provide approaches which may work in other areas.

We hope we have shown in this chapter that every organization needs a slightly different approach to introducing KIM. However, we also hope we have highlighted what can frequently go wrong with KIM programmes, and how you can avoid these pitfalls. This chapter has looked at what you need to think about at the start of any KIM activity. The next four chapters look at specific types of KIM activity and how you can approach introducing them.

Further reading

Davenport, T. and Prusak, L. (1998) *Working Knowledge*, Harvard Business School Press.

Handy, C. (1976) *Understanding Organizations*, Penguin.

Schopflin, K. (2015) Success in Knowledge Management: against the revolutionary approach. In *Proceedings of the SLA Annual Conference 2015*, Special Libraries Association.

Seely Brown, J. and Duguid, P. (2000) *The Social Life of Information*, Harvard Business School Press.

Chapter 3

Information management and governance

Every organization needs to keep track of the content it has created. Yet most organizations' information assets are stored in multiple locations with little corporate control over what is kept where, and for how long. Even where one or two appropriately structured central systems cover key functions (for example, customer relationship management in sales, stock control in retail, or case management in law), it is likely that staff have access to and use many other data repositories in the course of their work. And the number of places where staff might store the information they create is only increasing. This chapter is about the issues KIM professionals need to consider when managing expressed knowledge: where it can be found, what risks it carries, and what you can do about them. In an increasingly chaotic world of written information, what can an information manager do to provide structure?

The key issue for workers who create or require information comes under the headings 'findability' and 'putability'. This is covered by the questions 'Can I find the information I need to do my job?' and 'Where do I put the information I have created?' The answer to both questions should be the same, so that staff can access information created by each other. In our post-manufacturing world, most organizations' largest output is collections of words and numbers held in Word documents, Excel spreadsheets and PowerPoint presentations. Where they end up depends on how the issues of findability and putability are addressed. This is the essential task of the information manager and one that has only increased with the quantity of explicit information. One of the authors of this book once overheard a senior policy-maker complain that their e-mail inbox was full of essential policy, strategy and position papers that she needed to read, but she was too busy writing other such papers to do so. Over time, not just the quantity but the number of locations of recorded corporate information has increased. And as more items are saved in shared repositories, the more difficult it is to find useful content and ensure it is kept for the right amount of time.

As mentioned in Chapter 1, the corporate world began to express concerns about IM in the 1990s. Company executives were worried that they could not find their own information, which they recognised was one of their few tangible assets to increase in value over time. KPMG's Hawley Committee report (1995, 11) aimed to identify what good quality information should look like and the measures organizations should take to achieve it. They suggested that information should be:

- available in appropriate amounts and appropriately accessible
- timely and reliable
- flexible – easy to gather and manipulate
- consistently recorded over time.

Surprisingly, given the climate of corporate freedom of the time, the committee's recommendations were most concerned about the risks of poor information control. They advocated that businesses should ensure appropriate information access, retention and accuracy, through activities like:

- controlling permissions
- creating audit trails
- generating metadata
- controlling versions of documents
- assigning ownership to key pieces of information
- developing strategic asset registers to ensure key information is identified
- developing retention schedules to ensure information is only kept for as long as it needs to be.

Although it is thought that the Hawley Report largely failed in its attempt to encourage businesses to adopt better IM, it did articulate the need for it. Since then, within the fields of management, information technology, records management and library and information studies many attempts have been made to identify what organizations should do to manage their information better. Elizabeth Orna, one of the leading writers on the topic, emphasized the importance of IM to enable organizations to make the best use of their assets by making them visible and manageable (2004, 9). For her, IM concerns:

* acquiring, storing and making information accessible
* developing resources which enable users to add their knowledge
* ensuring resources are appropriate to meet changes in workplace environment
* reflecting organizational exchanges with the outside world
* using IT appropriately and innovatively to support these processes
* making lessons of experience accessible as an information resource.

This last point indicates that for Orna the line between information and knowledge was artificial. Expressed knowledge in documents and databases, and tacit knowledge in the practices, habits and expertise of staff are equally important and feed into each other. She advised developing not just repositories, but practices which enable corporate knowledge to be accessed in the course of all operations, processes and transactions in the working of an organization. Good IM practice would emerge from the interaction of staff with the tools made available to them, and their motivation for using them to record their information.

More prosaically, Jela Webb (2008, 23) suggested that information is managed well when it is:

* efficiently identified and stored
* accessible at all points during its existence and by all relevant employees
* used responsibly with regard to compliance
* managed like an asset equivalent to land, staff and capital
* 'viewed as the currency of competitiveness'
* prized and respected.

She added that information should be available at the right time, in the right location and to the right people. For her, good quality information demonstrates its provenance (how accurate and authoritative it is), its context (how it can be used) and its worth to the organization which owns it (48–9).

What Orna and Webb envisaged is the ideal for organizations to ensure that they do not waste or risk their assets. For many years, organizations felt that top-down control was the only means of doing this. But despite many attempts at control, most organizations are imperfect in their IM practices. This chapter aims to outline the challenges an information manager is likely to meet in the workplace and the best ways that they can rise to meet them.

Information and data repositories

As a knowledge or information manager, you will be required to oversee a myriad of repositories of data, information and perhaps knowledge. These will range from network drive file shares to databases and will be in varied states of control, order and structure.

Such repositories will present in three states of existence: structured, semi-structured and unstructured.

Structured repositories

A structured repository has a considered architecture. It labels stored information logically following set naming conventions. The items within might share a set of metadata labels or classification terms, with like items bearing the same names or categories. The structure should be comprehensible to all users so they know what is to be found within a particular named folder, for example. In a folder structure, the logic should continue within the folder; sub-folders and documents should continue to be named consistently and offer no surprises to those browsing.

Semi-structured repositories

Some repositories manage successfully to have a logical top level structure but beneath are buckets of unstructured information or documents. This might happen where the contents have outgrown an initially simple structure, where an internal structure was not enforced or where a pragmatic approach was taken that a simple structure would allow some measure of findability and stood more chance of users adhering to it.

Unstructured repositories

Very simply, this is a repository where no rules or logic has been applied to the information stored within it. It is the electronic equivalent of a room full of random piles of paper.

Traditionally, IM has been the art of applying controls to organizational content and knowledge assets through the creation of structured repositories. KIM professionals are appointed to ease the discovery of the content the organization creates and help apply governance rules to it (for example, to ensure that personal data is not retained longer than it should be). As mentioned in Chapter 1, the modern workplace encourages staff to create and manage their own content. The challenge for the information manager is to encourage them to save it in such a way that it can be found by their colleagues. At times it can be difficult to convince them that the content they create belongs, after all, to their employer and not to themselves. And even where staff are willing, shared repositories, as with all information systems, remain a compromise. If they perfectly reflect an individual or single group's understanding of the world, they are likely to be challenging for other users. If they attempt to match the searching and naming behaviour of all staff, they will please nobody.

Ironically, poor findability compounds the problem of ever more dispersed repositories. When staff cannot access the information they need, they create their own local stores at department, team or even individual level. These may contain many of the same documents as each other, but probably not the most up-to-date versions. This is an undesirable outcome to an existing problem. To use an analogy, if you are searching for a needle in a haystack, it is advisable to reduce the haystack rather than add more needles. But few workers feel empowered to delete content from bloated shared repositories (such as network drives or cloud storage). If they like order and control, they are more likely to set up a micro-store for themselves than share in a corporate repository. Anecdotally, this behaviour is as prevalent among information professionals as other staff: while saving little in their shared information store, their own inboxes and team drives contain folder structures of perfect logic and consistency.

As with all aspects of KIM, people are key to how organizational information can be managed. Because the key problems concern how they act when they store and seek information, the theory of good IM often does not match actual behaviour. The last decade has seen many organizations attempt different organization-wide approaches to controlling their corporate information with limited success. As a response to this, some organizations prefer to allow staff to keep information in an entirely unstructured way, and rely on powerful search tools to surface content. They consider time spent training and persuading staff in good information practice a poor investment, with little likelihood of success. In the past, many organizations felt the worst outcome of not implementing proactive IM would be at worst a need to re-create information again. An increased awareness of data compliance needs, and fear of penalties for non-compliance, has made rules around data retention a higher priority. It is a challenge for organizations without rules for where staff should put their information to be able to delete data they no longer need. To remain compliant, they are most likely to need to impose automatic data deletion, which may be resented by staff. We don't assume that traditional top-down IM is right for every organization, but we think that all organizations need to consider the risks of their strategic information approach, and put mitigations in place.

The next section looks at the types of data repositories most organizations use, the problems they present, and what we consider to be the best approach for managing information

Types of repository

Hard data repositories

As mentioned above, most organizations have at least one central system containing the key data around their organizational core function. Large organizations with multiple activities are likely to have many of them. It is in these systems that structure can most easily be imposed. Workers know they have to fill out specific fields and a well-designed system should reflect daily processes and gather the information the organization needs. This type of IM is carried out by most organizations and, at its best, enables findability to perfectly mirror putability. As the data has an excellent structure it can be analysed and reported on to show performance and trends, and thus give managers of any organization a deep insight into its weak spots and new areas to focus on.

Ideally, your systems also have the capability of talking to each other. For example, you may hold a customer database with the names, contact details and, where appropriate, service needs of your users. Its primary purpose is to record what your clients were or are entitled to receive in return for their payment or other qualification. A software as a service company is likely also to have a component within its software which records permissions structures, enabling clients to access different parts of the product depending on qualifying criteria (such as subscription package). Ideally the two data points would be perfectly matched: the names and statuses of users would be recorded once and used across the two systems. However, it is quite likely that they work in isolation from each other.

One of the authors of this book worked in a company where the customer relationship management system recorded the business name of the customer and number of qualifying users, while the back-end module of the product recorded the names of users and their permissions. Any changes which happened in one system could only be recorded manually in the other. This meant, for example, that if the customer had reduced the number of users they paid for, and this was recorded on the customer relationship management system, the individuals would still have access until the changes were recorded in the product. This type of problem is common in small organizations typically using

Case study 3.1: Core organizational data

Organization A is a professional membership organization with an extremely large number of different membership categories, reflecting the complexity of the profession it represents and the needs of different members.

Its central membership system was used by contact centre staff to record enquiries, talk members through the process of signing up and record any changes in their professional career (which would affect what they paid in membership). In many cases, the needs of the enquirer were sufficiently complex that details could only be taken over the phone and a more senior member of staff needed to calculate the individual tariff. In addition, the structure of the profession had changed in response to wider policy initiatives, so over time the inherent structure of the database no longer accurately reflected the questions being asked of membership staff. Where the field names or menu choices did not match the member's details, staff were increasingly forced to use free-text fields to record individual circumstances. This not only made accurate reporting very difficult, but also widened the scope for error, or for inconsistent charging to be applied.

Moving to a new system was never going to be straightforward. Membership could last for a professional's entire career and, even if they let their membership lapse, records needed to be maintained for as long as they were alive. For reasons connected with the nature of the profession, the integrity of their membership data over the course of their careers was essential. Moreover, data analysis helped the organization track professional trends, enabling them to focus their services where they were needed better. Any new system needed to conform well enough with the existing one to enable consistency of information. Finally, the technical and cultural change for staff brought by a system implementation project would have a profound effect on the ability to deliver a smooth service.

When the decision was taken to invest in a new database, it was decided to capitalise on the change and address another issue considered to be a problem: the labour- and task-intensive nature of the membership process. It was felt that membership staff spent too long on data entry, which members would be better placed to input themselves. The repetitive nature of the task was considered to be a reason why staff turnover was so high – a long investment in training often only resulted in 12–18 months' work. A measure of self-service was therefore built into the project plan for the new system.

Unfortunately the competing aims of the project were not compatible because although the same information needed to be gathered, the pathway for internal staff and end-users was not the same. Although the fields in the new system better reflected members' needs, it was more time-consuming for staff to enter information and few members wanted to input the data required when signing up themselves. Ultimately, the mistake was to allow an efficiency idea based on aspiration rather than experience – self-service – to outweigh the needs of the workers. Because it lost sight of the informational imperatives – for data capture to match the needs of the organization, and make staff more efficient – the project has generally been considered a failure.

micro-services. The micro-services approach seeks the best product on the market to carry out an individual task, usually through an economical cloud-based application. It offers freedom for staff to work with the best technology for the job, but it results in data being held in multiple repositories. However, dispersed data is not restricted to small organizations. For political or historical reasons, many organizations run multiple central systems repeating corporate data in more or less accurate ways and incompatibly with each other. Until the 21st century, most universities had entirely separate systems for managing student registration and other services such as libraries, accommodation or pastoral care. The latter therefore had to re-enter student data from scratch, and flags against student graduation (for example, unpaid library fines) would not automatically show up in the registration and examination systems. Organizations formed after takeovers and mergers are particularly likely to have overlapping systems repeating information inconsistently.

The answer to this problem comes under the label master data management. Developed specifically for the commercial sector and with customer data in mind in particular, it was concerned with 'creating a single source approach for management of master data based on high standards of quality and governance serving the entire business' (Cervo and Allen, 2011, 1). A good master data management system holds essential data in a separate system and maintains it as an accurate record. It can be shared with other systems requiring it on a field by field basis, ensuring only necessary fields are shared. It therefore allows information to be created once and used multiple times, maintained accurately in a single place, and only shared where necessary. Not every organization is willing or able to take the master data management approach to their core data. To do so means confronting issues of control ('this is my department's data') and fear ('my data is too sensitive to hold outside my function's system'). So hard data can be managed sub-optimally.

Moreover, as case study 3.1 demonstrates, even a well-managed central system is likely to fall out of step with the reality it is supposed to represent. The more highly structured the data, the better its reporting capability, but also the more restricted its flexibility in recording nuance and development. If you cannot fit an important instance of what you need to record into your existing data structures, then it will either go unrecorded, or be recorded in an unstructured way, which does not show up in reporting. Arguably, the harder the data, the less descriptive it is. This means that hard data repositories can tell us information of only limited depth.

A well-structured central repository is a key element to corporate IM but, as indicated, the structure can become out of date, and is unlikely to encompass all corporate data. Ideally, systems should be designed with daily use in mind. Information managers are ideally placed to help match the structure of the information to the daily tasks of those using it. Employees will use a repository if it is well designed and easy to use. It can be a challenge for IM departments to gain access to large-scale database implementations, which are often expensive and commissioned at a high level, but it is worth trying. We recommend working with service managers to identify the relationship between optimal ways of working and how information should be added. In this way, IM professionals who understand how data is structured and how people work can be the bridge between the system procurement and its ultimate users. Hard data repositories are only a small part of organizational information, but they at least should be well organized.

Soft data repositories

Separate from highly encoded, structured data recorded on large databases are organizational repositories containing hundreds or thousands of individual documents. These might be network drives, whether shared across the organization, within a team or personal to an individual. They might be other team-based repositories such as team sites, or other corporate stores, such as electronic document and records management (EDRM) systems. Sometimes these repositories are held within central systems, for example, correspondence attached to case management systems. In addition, there is an increasing quantity of unstructured information held in corporate messaging systems like Skype for Business or Slack, or in comments on corporate social media applications or intranet systems. And a huge quantity of corporate data is held in e-mail. Because of the latter's ubiquity, we address it separately.

In most organizations, soft repositories contain the largest quantity of corporate data and that with the highest risks attached to it. One approach to tackling it is to implement a single corporate system to manage this data, with more or less strict controls against communicating or storing information outside it. Some organizations design their central system of customer or case management to hold all external correspondence, including e-mails, and all-staff communication, whether formal or informal. This approach enables organizations to maintain control and creates a single place to manage document retention and deletion. A well-designed system makes it possible to organize otherwise unstructured data: e-mails and correspondence relating to a particular case are kept within that particular area and with any associated metadata, enabling it to be found, and deleted if necessary, within the appropriate time frame. Every application within the system should be perfectly compatible with every other one.

However, such monolithic systems can cause problems of their own. Centralised systems tend to offer a suite of components covering different corporate activities, but rarely do any of them do as well as software designed to do a single thing. Staff may resent having to use a module in a centralised system when they are familiar with using a specialised application, with better designed features (as if in acknowledgement of this, few systems come without the ability to export data to Excel). Faced with systems they do not enjoy using, users find alternatives. For example, if they do not like the social media element of a central system, they are more likely to use external applications, perhaps from their own phone. This creates greater risks for the management of corporate information than allowing staff to use a range of products.

Moreover, not every instance of important corporate activity may fit into the existing structures of a central system, however much management may wish them to. An extreme example of this was seen in a small marketing company which resisted issuing staff with their own PCs for years. Every PC or laptop in the business was dedicated to a current project and could be worked on by any member of staff as they needed to contribute. But the system had to be abandoned so that staff could work on general business development and planning, or to develop uncommissioned projects. Law firms which use legal case management systems attached to payment systems encounter similar problems. While managers would like 100% of staff time to be accountable to a particular billable case, staff may do valuable work which does not fit the billing structure.

Finally, single monolithic systems tie organizations into proprietary software, which the vendor may or may not wish to continue to develop, regardless of whether it undergoes takeover or merger. Even the example of application compatibility may not apply in these instances. Microsoft SharePoint implementations proliferated in the first 15 years of the 21st century, yet never supported consistent metadata across its suite of products. Companies that had invested in SharePoint found it difficult to transfer existing information when the latest version came out, particularly if they had customised it to meet their needs. For 'Microsoft Houses' (those who implemented MS Windows operating systems) in the early 21st century, SharePoint seemed like the answer to all of their data needs, but in reality offered no solution to the problems of managing soft data.

The next few sections look at some particular aspects of soft data. As will become apparent, the authors feel one-size-fits-all systems probably aren't the counter to the proliferation of soft data repositories. It is a challenge to maintain compatibility over dispersed systems, but in the modern world total control is impossible. There are simply too many options for staff to work outside central systems. Far preferable is to educate staff about their responsibilities over the information they create, and provide them with the tools that most suit the function and culture of their activity. Below we expand on this approach, but first we wanted to look at one particular area of soft information that dominates the current workplace, and its alternatives.

E-mail

Despite multiple predictions of its death over the years (for example Vascarello, 2009) e-mail remains the typical record of most daily business activity. For the information manager, e-mail offers perfect functionality for poor IM practice:

* Information is held in individually siloed repositories.
* An extra copy is made each time an e-mail is sent.
* New copies of attachments proliferate.
* As a legacy system, the only structure it offers is by person's name.
* It encourages information to be shared between small numbers of people on a single occasion.
* It offers no easily accessible corporate memory.

Yet it remains the place where, at the time of writing (2018), most people choose to do business, with their inbox operating as their to-do list, their business prioritisation platform and their main form of communication. Research at Loughborough University (2013) – for the full research see Marulanda-Carter (2013) – found a link between the quantity and arrival of e-mail and rising levels of stress throughout the working day. We know receiving e-mails makes us stressed, yet we continue to send them. E-mail platforms' unique combination of accessible storage with fast communication is irresistible. And the fact that it remains popular when faster options, such as chat (see below) is available, shows that its ability to time-shift (I will give you my answer in my time, not yours) is desirable. In addition to having, at best, semi-structured repositories of documents, most organizations have vast archives of e-mails, which may or may not record important business decisions. Case study 3.2 shows that its ubiquity makes deletion both entirely necessary, but also a very difficult decision to make.

In the early part of the 21st century, the typical IM approach involved compelling staff to save business e-mails in corporate systems (such as EDRM

Case study 3.2: The legacy of email

Organization B is a public sector body, which implemented an e-mail archiving policy, whereby any e-mail over a month old would be removed from immediate access in current inboxes and instead be archived in a corporate data store. Staff could retrieve e-mails from within their inbox, if they had not deleted them, as a stub was kept, but content of the e-mail would not be found in a mailbox search. Staff were encouraged to save e-mails into an EDRM system, which had an add-on enabling e-mails to be saved directly from the user's inbox. However, the interaction between the e-mail and EDRM systems was cumbersome and time-consuming and many staff did not use it.

As a result all but the most recent e-mails were unavailable to staff, although in corporate terms all e-mails were kept indefinitely, in a largely unstructured way. Because e-mails were archived automatically, rather than being deleted by the user, it could not be assumed that everything in the archive was ephemeral. Because it was known that significant numbers of staff did not save e-mails to the EDRM system, it could not be assumed that information was captured elsewhere. The risk that the e-mail archive contained records of business decisions and quite possibly legal documents meant it could not simply be deleted.

As a first stage of the e-mail archiving project, it was agreed with the internal audit department that, leaving aside current open investigations and legal holds, all e-mails over seven years old could be deleted. As a second stage, this seven-year repository was moved onto a new platform, which had far greater search capability and enabled e-mails to be found. A set of rules was developed to allow some e-mails to be deleted immediately within the repository and all others on a rolling basis of seven years. Staff were by now using a new e-mail system to which a similar set of rules could be applied. A rolling two years' worth of e-mails were to be kept within their own mailboxes. As a start, the current archive is now reduced to seven years. The introduction of collaborative workspaces is hoped to reduce the reliance on e-mail as a means of communication. And the bulk that is left will now be searchable.

systems or cloud repositories). Although specific tools were acquired to enable this to happen, on the whole staff preferred to keep their information in their own inbox. Many managers attempted to discourage this through imposing mailbox space limits or automatic deletion, with limited success in encouraging use of the central repository. Staff like e-mail as a corporate tool (even where, in their private lives, they are far more likely to use a social media messaging app). If we want to discourage staff from using it, we have to offer them ways of managing their most important information with a comparable ease of use.

Traditional IM strategies attempt to solve the 'e-mail problem' through central controls and providing a single alternative channel. The sensible IM professional recognises e-mail's multiple functions and their organizations' diversity, and offers staff as many different tools as possible. Alternatives are adopted, particularly if given support and used by senior staff. After all, any communications method requires both a sender a receiver. And experience shows that given the opportunity, staff are happy not to have to deal with a constant influx of e-mail.

Here are six alternatives to e-mail:

cloud-based documents, which enable workers to collaborate without sending even links to the documents back and forth by e-mail (although they can set this up to send and receive notifications when a change is made)

chat, which works for ephemeral conversations that don't need a memory

an intranet, which is a much better channel than e-mail for corporate messages and company-wide information

well-designed self-service channels, which reduce one-to-one transactions carried out by e-mail

training, which if relevant and timely can reduce the number of individual questions asked

social channels and discussion forums, which create a collaborative space ideal for ephemeral discussion (more on this in the next chapter).

Chat

Most organizations now have some form of instant business messaging to enable workers to communicate short written messages online. How far it is adopted depends on the organization. One of the authors of this book has worked in organizations where users routinely use a hybrid of e-mail and chat to manage their information, communication and knowledge. Chat has a place between unrecorded communication and e-mail for semi-formal business processes. Some chat functions come with the ability to record and track all conversation, which then becomes part of the corporate record, albeit one not easy to access. Many managers of organizations choose to automatically delete any chat conversations after a specified time period. Where this occurs, chat is clearly not the right place to record core business decisions. Whichever control is put in place, staff need to understand what happens to their chats after they close down for the day.

Intranets

By 'intranet' we mean an organization's internal channel for providing authoritative, rarely changing information useful to staff. In the next chapter, we discuss social forms of online space, and Chapter 5 looks at knowledge repositories which are often hosted on intranets. Here we refer to the intranet as a broadcast communication channel covering the information needed by all or most employees in addition to the specifics of their job. It is often considered outside the scope of IM, yet the authors have both worked on corporate intranets and agree that it is a key to good practice. If the right information is on the intranet, then a whole strafe of IM is already accomplished on employees' behalf. A well-designed intranet answers all the questions staff ask in the course of doing their jobs, so they do not need to e-mail support departments. It gives them access to authoritative documents so they do not need to store them locally. It provides access to self-service functions to enable them to carry out tasks such as booking leave, claiming expenses and managing their technical needs. If structured around the needs of users, rather than those of the department which owns the information, an intranet should provide a model of providing just enough information at just the right time.

If as a knowledge manager you manage the corporate intranet, or work with the corporate communications team to do so, you can use it as a channel of communication to reduce e-mail traffic. In one organization one of the authors of this book recognised that attempting to encourage staff to send fewer e-mails was futile when they received so many corporate communications by e-mail. As is so often the case, senior staff did not want to rely on the intranet to send messages because, as a 'pull' communications channel, they might not be read. With the support of executive-level staff, the author managed to persuade managers gradually to reduce corporate e-mail messages and daily updates, and eventually cease sending them altogether, except for a small number of agreed messages. It was made clear to users that it was their responsibility to check the intranet, and their fault if they missed any key activities because they had not done so. An internet central media platform was supported and pushed to the business with a network of champions to encourage and build momentum. None of these initiatives alone completely eradicated the issue of e-mail overload but analytics suggested that e-mail traffic reduced over time.

The two key challenges of corporate intranets, and the reason why they are often used sub-optimally, are access and use. To remain user-focused, concise and authoritative, the intranet should have central control. But too much control, or too unwieldy a method of updating information, hampers staff attempts to update it. Once out of date, intranets are no longer trusted as information sources, and staff start to keep local copies of policies, and to e-mail individual departments for the information they need. So, staff need to be able to update pages, even while editorial processes are clear and staff know what they have to do to submit information and when. The second problem concerns how to encourage staff to visit an intranet in the first place. Both authors of this book have used a daily all-staff e-mail as a means of enticing staff, with the hope that it could be discontinued in time, with some success. Providing access to self-service systems can also be an incentive, as staff all want to be paid and take their annual leave. Ultimately, staff will use the intranet if it contains information they need or want. Analytics can be a tool to work out what these things are. If used well, the corporate intranet is part of the solution to IM problems and a civilised, well organized location in the chaos of corporate information.

Self-service systems

Self-service systems deserve an extra mention of their own. As noted above, the key to IM is matching the information recorded to how people are going to look for it. Well-designed self-service systems ideally match process to information capture. If the journey the employee is led on matches their needs, it should eliminate one-to-one communications. A good system should help staff understand the information they need to provide, which then matches the information needs at the other end of the transaction. Some organizations use self-service to siphon off a bulk of queries, leaving a long tail of one-to-one transactions which need to be managed by e-mail, telephone or in person. However, one of the authors is developing a human resources (HR) self-service platform which aims to manage all HR-related transactions in employees' working lives. The structure is based on knowledge needs identified from calls made to the existing call centre and will be adaptable as needs change over the course of time. Once implemented, staff should be able to manage all their own transactions (for example, not just annual leave, but special leave) with minimal need for one-to-one interactions. Information managers may not be the first people asked when self-service systems are procured or designed, but their ability to match information needs to information outputs can make the difference between a good and bad platform design. As mentioned in Chapter 1, you may find poorly resourced support departments delighted to have your input and we encourage you to think laterally about how IM skills can create efficiencies in areas like this.

A word about controls

Although IM is ultimately about control, we can't emphasise enough that if you use control as your main mechanism for compliance you are unlikely to be successful. Users can always find methods to by-pass controls on how they keep, label and destroy their data, and the risks are even higher if they choose to do this outside corporate systems. This is not to say that controls are not useful checking points. They are certainly a suitable way to encourage good behaviour. But the will for good behaviour needs to be present first.

We think the best way to illustrate this is by providing some real-life examples of corporate controls which have not succeeded or, worse, have increased the risk of information being lost, kept for too long or otherwise mismanaged:

> *the policy-writing unit which banned shared subject files*: an unstructured box of useful material was assembled for each paper as it was being written and then disposed of once it was published, which happily removed the need for storage and indexing; however, because subject experts often needed to write on the same topics again, they started to keep their own micro-repositories on their personal profile or desktop
>
> *the company which banned e-mail of any non-work-related nature and made it clear that mailboxes were being monitored*: increasingly, staff had smartphones and communicated both work and non-work issues using personal e-mail and private social media outlets such as Twitter Direct Message or WhatsApp
>
> *the organization which restricted the size of personal drives and inboxes, but unofficially relaxed them on request for anyone at director level or above (including the director of IM)* causing resentment and similar requests from more junior staff
>
> *the centrally controlled intranet with insufficient staff to upload new policies as they became available*: staff created local repositories for up-to-date policies and e-mailed them to colleagues when asked for them.

As indicated in the section on e-mail above, controls are effective when they remind workers to adopt behaviour which they already understand as better for everybody. As has probably become clear, we think that too much control infantilises staff rather than empowering them and pushes them into sub-optimal behaviour. We think there are better ways to encourage staff to think about where the information they create should be stored and how it should be communicated.

Key points of advice for good information management

These are some guidelines for managing information well:

- Provide alternative communication and collaboration portals and remember that different groups choose to work in different ways.
- Gain support at senior level and persuade senior managers to lead by example.
- Gain access to as many different repositories and communications channels as possible and offer advice on risk mitigation for each one.
- Never implement a company-wide solution and expect it to be adopted by everyone.
- Develop pilot user groups to try new channels, track activity through analytics and show the business that change can be achieved.
- Use training to remind people of their options, and what they can be used for.
- Use intranet or internet pages to provide key information which changes slowly.
- Encourage people to send links to centrally stored information rather than attachments.
- Support and drive internal social media channels.
- Build a network of champions around the organization to set examples and support cultural change.

These may seem like a fairly lightweight set of guidelines, but they are achievable and likely to gain engagement in a way that top-down controls do not. This is not to say that having rules and guidance around IM is futile. We feel that the list of points above is a toolkit that you can use to support policies, strategy and training. The next section looks at this in depth.

Governance and policies

Having made clear that central control is not the answer to good IM, this section outlines the roles and nature of governance and policies and how they can be used successfully. In the early 21st century, the starting point for many organizations embracing IM was to put in place a suite of strategies, policies and guidance documents, backed up by corporate file plans and retention schedules. We outline the main varieties of document below, but we urge caution. Having the best suite of policy documents in the world will not change your users' behaviour. The more detailed and specific the instructions as to what staff can and cannot do, the less likely they are to read them, never mind act on them. In the rapidly evolving post-document world of collaborative spaces and informal information-sharing repositories, it is even harder to enforce standardised behaviour. Most organizations with poor IM practice do have policies in place, it is simply that staff do not follow them.

In many cases the ideas behind information policies were not bad but they were often applied inflexibly, often on the wrong repositories or targeting the wrong users or team. As the examples in the section 'A word about controls' show, policies are often upheld inconsistently or merely serve to ensure that users find ways around them. The last two decades have taught us that governance documents created and shared with an unwilling body of knowledge and information consumers tend to be entirely ignored. We continue to believe that policies are useful, as they provide a reference point when there is doubt over what people should do. They allow poor practice to be tackled and the authorisation of remedial action. But they can only ever be a starting point.

Data protection and corporate policies

In contradiction to the above, it has never been a better time to establish good information governance through policies. At the time of writing, data governance has a particularly high profile in countries that trade within or with the European Economic Area. GDPR requires that anyone sharing data within this data protection regime does not simply adhere to the principles of good data management, but provides evidence for it as well. A simplified summary of previous data protection legislation would say that organizations need to look after any data they hold or use which relates to an identifiable living person. They should:

- only gather and keep data required to provide services
- keep data securely, accurately and only for as long as necessary
- communicate to people what is held on them
- not transport data to a territory working under a different data protection regime.

Under GDPR, organizations need to provide written evidence that they adhere to these principles and that data protection is built into everything they do. To comply, they need to demonstrate that data principles are as important as any other project or business process outcome, that staff receive the training they need to ensure they understand their responsibilities, and that data breaches are recorded and acted on at the highest level. Above all, organizations need to show that they know what personal data they hold, who they share it with and how long they keep it for. The penalties for organizations that do not comply are fines at a much higher scale than those imposed in many territories operating under the previous data protection regime.

The policies outlined below, therefore, are a crucial part of establishing data compliance. This does not in fact contradict our observations about the failures of information policy in the past. The UK Information Commissioner, Elizabeth Denham, has made it clear that having policies is not enough (Information Commissioner's Office, 2017). In a speech to the UK's leading accountancy body she said:

> It's about moving away from seeing the law as a box ticking exercise, and instead [working] on a framework that can be used to build a culture of privacy that pervades an entire organization. . . . If a business can't show that good data protection is a cornerstone of their practices, they're leaving themselves open to a fine or other enforcement action that could damage [their] bank balance or business reputation.

If they wish to work within this data protection regime, organizations must show that policies are more than just pieces of paper, but result in behaviour. We thoroughly endorse this as an approach.

Types of policy documents

Information management policy and strategy documents

This type of document is usually a very high-level document outlining how an organization expects its staff to manage information. Signed off policies carry the authority of the most senior people in the organization and, if possible, most of the key business users too. It is usual to think of a policy document as the top level document, with the organization's strategy emerging out of this. Orna (1999, 9–10) makes the distinction between a policy document, which defines principles and overall priorities for information, and a strategy document, which is 'the detailed expression of information policy in terms of objectives, targets, and actions to achieve them, for a defined period ahead'. The one is general, the other is more likely to have time-based objectives. In reality, they are both starting documents, and there can be no advantage in having too many top level documents. In our opinion, a policy document can be important, but good information behaviour should be incorporated into all the strategies that lie below it. The owner of good information behaviour should be the business owner, not the information manager. So we would advise restricting yourself to a top level IM policy document, whose general approach is incorporated into all business strategies.

Information strategy documents are usually compiled by people in senior IM roles, in consultation with the managers within the business and looking at best practice documents from other organizations. Consulting staff demonstrates to them that you intend to base the strategy on their business priorities. However, you may find the final document cannot represent everyone's needs and there is no guarantee that staff will apply the strategy in their own area of adoption. Middle managers of important operational areas may resent interference in policies and strategies they consider to be entirely their own. It is important to establish where your authority lies in constructing or advising on strategies: you want staff to manage information well, but you are not there to tell them how to do their job.

Typically, information policies contain sections such as:

* *definitions*: 'information is considered any written material which records business activities'
* *scope*: 'we consider this to cover all the information created in the course of our company's work'
* *attitude*: 'information should be considered as an asset equivalent to budget or equipment'
* *approach*: 'information should be made available as default and only stored in restricted areas if necessary'
* *aspiration*: 'all the information on our intranet should be accurate, relevant and up to date'
* *vision*: 'by the year X we aim to have all records of business decisions stored within a single repository'.

No one would argue with any of this, but the way information policies are put into action is key. A good way of judging a policy or strategy document's success is to consider whether it can be used to solve problems. For example, an information manager tackling out-of-date content on their intranet could draw the appropriate section of the information policy to the attention of the content owner. The authority of the policy may carry weight and encourage the content owner to act when they would otherwise have ignored such a request.

Another good method to incorporate information policies into day-to-day behaviour is to use them as a starting point for local procedures. For example, an information policy document may state, 'We take responsibility for all personal data we hold.' This could be incorporated into more detailed strategies for information systems. The systems must be planned with good information security and risk management in place. The next stage after this is to ensure that the strategy is carried into guidance documents and training. In this way, policy can drive staff behaviour. Policies do not themselves affect organizational behaviour, but they are essential to support your IM activities.

This type of approach is central to better data management. Everyone who creates and manages information has responsibility for information behaviour. An IM policy can state principles and good practice, but implementation only comes through the policies and procedures which underlie all the activities that take place in the organization. Identifying information asset owners helps make this happen.

Information audits

Information audits establish the information assets an organization holds. They would seem to be essential for anyone trying to ensure that organizations do not lose their essential data and do not keep information for longer than they need to. They can also establish the authority of your information, and how valuable it is for decision-making. Unfortunately, they can be time-consuming and become out of date as soon as they are completed. Arguably, the emergence of social networking tools for business activities creates so many repositories that a comprehensive audit is impossible.

You can automate aspects of the audit process, for example by distributing online forms rather than holding interviews. You may need to follow up to ensure comprehensivity, but the less burden you put on staff at the information-gathering stage the better. You may want to focus on key staff or processes, or those more likely to change quickly, such as special projects or new initiatives. When gathering data, consider its possible uses. One of the authors of this book was able to use knowledge maps created by a predecessor to support a KM portal. These had identified areas of skill and knowledge across the organization, so that he could facilitate exchange between those who were seeking information and those who had it. Always audit with a purpose.

An audit always needs to balance the depth of information you need against the ability to maintain accuracy. You need to concentrate on things that you can actually act on. It is tempting to produce a catalogue of information assets and ignore more dynamic information about information flows and the age of data in different departments. Some of your key business processes will bounce between different departments, and by tracking them you can identify areas of information risk. Our advice is to take a risk-based approach. Of course you should understand broadly what information your organization holds, but you cannot be expected to keep an up-to-date record of every information repository. Outline the most heavily used areas, and any containing personal data. If need be, encourage staff to use key systems for any high-risk activity and allow them to understand the risks of doing otherwise. But accept that a comprehensive record is impossible.

One of the authors conducted an information audit for a medium-sized professional services firm. It was a comprehensive attempt to map all the information, data, records and knowledge the organization held. The audit was carried out through a series of interviews with key administrators within each division or team and follow-up interviews with senior staff. Four members of staff undertook the work across an organization of 400, split into 5 main divisions.

Although the organization had an aspiration to encourage more knowledge-sharing, the outcome was unscoped and unclear even to participants. The result was a monster, reflecting far too much detail recorded during the interview process. In many cases individual record sets were detailed. It took the author three months to make sense of the data and to present it in a form that allowed the team to make recommendations. During the process users often ran out of time and patience for interviews and just gave access to their repositories to the audit team to explore and analyse themselves (although results were then subsequently validated).

These were the negative results of the information audit:

* The lack of a clear scope meant it took almost 12 months to complete the audit, during which team members left and the project came close to being stopped more than once.
* Too much information was collected and at too fine a level of granularity for it all to be used.
* Although the organization was very conservative and not undergoing much change, some findings were out of date before the audit finished.
* Because of the time the audit team members were taking up interviewing, they came close to alienating a number of key knowledge professionals in the organizations and had to work hard to ensure they stayed engaged in the process.

These were the positive results of the information audit:

* The author was able to build a comprehensive knowledge map of the

organization, which even two or three years later was accurate enough to form the basis of a new intranet structure.

* Although not a stated aim, the team responsible for data protection subject access requests was better able to find information requested from them.
* The results enabled a full review of the company's retention and destruction policy and aligned retention schedule. The company reduced both its paper and electronic records by nearly 40% and moved off-site another significant amount with destruction rules applied.
* A comprehensive business taxonomy was produced and a new file plan for the shared drive was created reflecting the new retention schedule.
* A number of potential compliance issues were identified and resolved, and information governance was significantly improved. All legacy data was given an appropriate owner and awareness of data risks was raised.
* On the back of the audit the KIM team was greatly expanded, and a new strategy was implemented.

Despite these benefits, the author would not undertake such a large and comprehensive audit again, certainly not without a more clearly defined scope, even in another slow-moving conservative organization. Most of the realised benefits could have been gleaned from a much briefer and less granular exercise, conducted by fewer staff and taking up less time from the organization.

File plans

The corporate file plan emerged as a means of structuring shared network drives and later EDRM systems. It was a type of taxonomy providing locations for documents to be saved. Its key aims were:

* to enable information to be found, because it was stored with other, similar information
* to prevent the duplication or re-creation of information, because it was all held in one easily accessible location
* to enable retention schedules to be applied, so that documents of a similar kind were deleted at the same time.

File plans often came with file and folder naming conventions although these were difficult to mandate and often ignored.

Despite many expensive projects to apply structure to corporate repositories, untamed folder structures or unused repositories abound in businesses. The more control there is when creating information, for example, insisting on a category before a document can be saved, the less the structured repository will be used. But the fewer controls applied, the less useful it is as a finding aid. This is not to say that good document storage and naming practices are pointless. Indeed, many people want to know the best place they can save their information so they do not need to worry about it anymore.

File plans and naming conventions work best in two types of organizational area. The first is where there is content common to all staff in the business. Managers repeat the same processes for their staff across the organization, for example:

- inducting new staff
- managing leave and absence
- dealing with compensation and benefits (or pay and reward)
- planning learning and development
- managing career development, performance and discipline
- managing staff exit policies for those who leave the company.

Ideally a controlled repository for information related to these areas perfectly reflects the findability and putability problem identified above, enabling managers to store the information within a structure that reflects what they need to do, and the information central HR functions need to gather.

The second type of organizational area where file plans and naming conventions work well is where there is a shared language and practice area. Corporate file plans traditionally used a faceted approach, where users were encouraged, or forced, to use the same breakdown of file headings across their functional area. When strictly imposed, it resulted in unused folders and a large body of 'miscellaneous' material, which did not fit the structure. File plans need to reflect the work of those using them. Any introspective or clearly defined closed team within an organization will be receptive to an information structure that reflects how they divide and describe their world. A good information manager will work with teams to identify the structure that suits them and advise on other governance issues such as retention.

File plans were seen as a KM solution as well as an IM one. The theory was that if everyone shared their information in a shared corporate structure, there would be more transparency and awareness, and less need for different departments to re-create their own documents (or save multiple versions of the same ones) in their own areas. At the time of writing, it is notable that some organizations have accepted that people prefer to save in team-based areas and are not attempting to impose corporate-wide functional structures. However, it is possible for information managers to apply information governance rules into these team spaces at the point they are created. The space may be team-based but any documentation can obey consistent automated retention rules appropriate to the types of documents being saved. It is still necessary for users to have a 'save place' but it is one they feel comfortable using and the perceived governance burden is less. It is yet to be seen how successful this approach will be using platforms such as Office 365 and G Suite, but it can only be an improvement on poorly used corporate repositories.

Retention schedules

Retention schedules, which defined sets of document or information types, and applied instructions for deletion, were seen as the great hope for controlling the ever-expanding quantity of data at the end of the 20th century. They were seen as particularly important in complying with data protection legislation because, if implemented, an organization could be sure they were not keeping personal data longer than necessary. However, they are a classic example of a type of policy document which has not had the intended effect on staff's behaviour. Most organizations hold information far older than their retention schedule tells them to. Here are some reasons why:

- Often running to thousands of lines, retention schedules were impossible to use and rarely opened by information creators.
- People might comply with retention schedule specifications for records held in certain formats, for example, hard copy files, but not with e-mail or anything held in informal repositories.
- They could not ensure that corporate information was not being held on personal drives, laptops, home devices, personal e-mail accounts or private social media.
- Increasingly, the notion of information deletion became redundant: people became used to information existing indefinitely and being findable through search tools.
- It became far too easy to create too much information in far too many places.

Retention schedules originated in a hard copy world where destruction of documents created space on shelves, in archive boxes and in warehouses (although note that document storage companies usually charge more to destroy files than to store them). Today, online storage space is cheap. It could be argued that the ever-increasing proliferation of information in our repositories makes deletion even more important in the digital world. The less information you hold, the easier it is to find the important things. But the financial argument for data deletion has become less powerful as cheap cloud storage space has become available. Compliance is a far greater motivator.

We think there is still a role for guidance around content types and how long they should be kept for, although you probably don't want to call it a retention schedule. There is also definitely a place for automated deletion. As mentioned above, the move from centralised document management to dispersed cloud repositories may provide opportunities to remove the burden from the user. For example, any Google Drive enables retention terms to be applied to the whole drive when it is set up. If you plan your implementation properly, you can ensure that large categories of documents automatically have retention applied to them. The key challenge is encouraging people to choose the right location to save their content in to begin with. It was said that the ideal EDRM system was the one that generated automatic metadata governing how a document was classified and when it should be deleted. This was rarely achieved but could be a possibility with more dispersed drive-based structures, if they are set up and managed well.

Information asset registers

Information asset registers are typically lists of the most important or largest information sets within the organization, identifying an owner and some responsibilities attached to this status. They should ensure key information is well structured and findable, up to date and accurate, and not kept for longer than needed. Information asset registers were once part of the audit, file plan, and retention and destruction suite of documents owned by records and information managers, but were rarely adopted by the business as a whole. Owners often failed to identify themselves as information asset owners, or failed to act on their responsibilities. Faced with lack of adoption, some departments chose simply to identify individual systems or applications as assets and at least be able to manage them from a security point of view, even if the information held within them might cover a range of different risks, content types and optimal retention periods.

Yet information asset registers could be the key to spreading responsibility for good information behaviour throughout the business. Information asset owners should be managers of key functions within the organization, not technical systems. Operational managers may not want information responsibilities but they should be concerned about the information related to the function they manage. The manager of your SalesForce implementation may be in IT, but the information asset owner should be the head of sales. It should matter to them that they have accurate and findable sales information and they can be made to understand the reputational or financial risks if data is found to be kept for too long or insecurely. Generally speaking, we don't advocate using the stick over the carrot. However, this is one case where reminding staff of data protection law and potential fines may be useful in encouraging their concern about data retention and security. It can be a challenge to encourage operational managers to engage. It is worth reminding them that responsibilities and rights go hand in hand. If the information function team has responsibility for an information asset, they should also have control over how the data is kept and for how long. Would they really like it if their staff saw information disappear or be moved to another location without warning? Far more desirable is that the operational manager owns responsibility for both, albeit with advice and guidance from the information manager.

Information asset registers can be a very useful way to focus on risk. To be fully compliant with data protection legislation, organizations should know that they do not keep personal data any longer than they need to. Good IM helps this to happen, but we accept that it is impossible to control all organizational data on all possible platforms. If you have mapped the assets which carry risks, because of their personal or sensitive nature, or because of their strategic or commercial importance, you can focus your most stringent information controls on these areas. If you also train staff on the importance of using the right repository for the right type of information, you are a good way towards implementing information governance which stands a chance of adoption.

Recommended approaches

It is probably clear that the authors think the key to good IM is working with people to align good information behaviour with the outcomes they want themselves in their work. We don't underestimate the difficulty of engaging staff in caring about their organization's information. It may even be the case that the issues we have outlined above are not on the corporate radar. Cheap storage space, good search tools and a lack of fear of the consequences of compliance have made many chief executive officers relaxed about how their information is managed. Even organizations aware of the issue will point to failed attempts to implement IM in the past and accept that chaos is a necessary by-product of the modern data and information environment.

However, an increased awareness of data compliance needs, and fear of penalties for non-compliance, has made data retention and discovery a higher priority. Information managers can take this opportunity to show that knowing about your information is useful to an organization. Even after current concerns about data protection have become less of a priority, it must be an advantage to an organization to know what they hold and where they can find it. And if they do not care about personal data risks, then they should care about business continuity and commercial sensitivity.

It is not all about people, of course. Case study 3.2 shows that we are not resistant to automating IM where it is appropriate and does not adversely affect employees' working life. In fact, we would be the first to say that if you can make IM easier for employees through technological tools then you should do that even if your organization has engaged with IM and employees understand their responsibilities over the information they create. We also think that good taxonomical rules and data structures are essential, but they should be specific to the type of data or user group, match their language and be easy to apply.

We have spent a long time discussing IM, an area that some knowledge professionals feel is tangential to an essentially people-centred practice. However, it covers the most tangible part of a company's knowledge assets and therefore is the easiest discipline to show results. It is also the area information professionals are most likely to be called to work in, and the area they may naturally gravitate towards. Nevertheless, we hope we have shown that the key to good IM is engagement with people. The next few chapters look at the softer side of KIM, at how we can encourage people to collaborate to share their knowledge and to leave their knowledge where it can be found again.

Further reading

Orna, E. (1999) *Practical Information Policies*, Gower.
Orna, E. (2004) *Information Strategy in Practice*, Gower.
Webb, J. (2008) *Strategic Information Management: a practitioner's guide*, Chandos.

Chapter 4

Communities and knowledge-sharing

While the previous chapter concentrated on tangible artefacts of KIM, this chapter looks at practices centred around people. These are perhaps the most difficult to define, implement and gauge success. As the first chapter described, KM originated as a people-centred area of study and it is only over time that it has become associated with tangible systems. Indeed, some consider the knowledge held inside people's heads to be essentially unmanageable. This area of KM, therefore, largely concerns methods of encouraging the exchange of knowledge between people. This might be in a more or less formal manner and as far as the practice of KM is concerned may have different levels of intervention. Most of our examples will be around online collaboration spaces, but we also address face-to-face knowledge-sharing.

In this chapter we discuss a range of different approaches to sharing knowledge, broadly defined as communities of practice. These are groups formed in the course of negotiating their way through a shared part of working life, non-work endeavour or common interest. They are considered to share a language, common practices and behavioural shortcuts, but may be unaware that they constitute a community of practice. As a knowledge manager, you may have a more or less formal role building, facilitating and recording such communities and their outputs. While the community of practice may already exist, you can add value by organizing events, providing and curating online tools, and helping to bring knowledge and learning from the community back into the organization.

Why would an organization support a community of practice? It is a cheap way (staff time allowing) of enabling staff to learn from each other and share information, not requiring classroom sessions, professional trainers or lots of one-to-one information transactions. The benefits are more than this: we potentially learn more in an ongoing process of engagement with our peers than from a one-off session within which knowledge is organized into discrete packages. This is not to say that classroom sessions are not valuable, but communities of practice provide a constant means of reinforcing and developing formally acquired knowledge and skills, and putting them into practice. Moreover, formal training represents an official version of practices, systems and skills. The learning carried out in a community of practice includes workarounds and shortcuts you will never learn in the classroom.

As theories of communities of practice emerged, some were sceptical that organizational structures would support them. In a KM-debunking article, T. D. Wilson (2002) said:

> If organizations were structured in such a way as to encourage the creation of 'communities' in which members owed allegiance only to one another and had the autonomy to develop their own ways of working [then] expertise might well then be shared. However, organizations are not like this and business organizations in particular are certainly not always like this.

However, when he discussed the subject again in 2005, he acknowledged that staff sharing a professional interest at a certain level in the organization might benefit more from sharing than from hoarding information, and might participate in online or face-to-face forums. He even observed that certain professions, such as education and medicine, have 'natural communities of practice' because collaboration is essential in achieving what they need to do (Wilson, 2005). In reality, communities of practice emerge whether or not the organization supports them, as we communicate with our peers and learn from them.

Wilson observes that organizational hierarchies may present barriers to communication across organizations, and that patterns of reward and job security may be a disincentive for workers to share what they consider to be their personal employee capital. In some organizations, some groups may feel all of their knowledge needs are already met by existing tools, and that they have nothing to gain from sharing knowledge. However, they may have much to offer other users. Other organizational areas (whether separated by hierarchy or territory) may be 'net importers' of knowledge. Knowledge-sharing tools could, therefore, be a corrective to an imbalance in the availability of knowledge and resources. The key challenges are, first, to reassure staff that they are not 'giving away' their intellectual capital when they share and, second, to encourage comfortably complacent employee groups to listen to the diverse voices from around the organization. The first challenge is ideally addressed by a culture where sharing is rewarded. The second can best be addressed by demonstrating the value of diverse content.

Knowledge-sharing tools struggle to prove return on investment. That investment might only be staff time and the use of an online or physical space. But even this might be considered entirely wasted if there is no evidence that providing it has enabled the organization to capitalise on knowledge-sharing. The things that community facilitators can prove, such as attendance or contributions, are only records of staff time spent, not of outcomes. The latter can only really be proven over time, by anecdote or, in extreme situations, in the avoidance or otherwise of crises. Although sharing on online communities is corporate communication at its most present, and provides a memory, it is difficult to prove that the content can be mined for future knowledge value. However, while difficult to measure, over time there should be tangible outputs from knowledge-sharing forums, such as:

* discussion and analysis of common issues
* solutions found to common problems
* best practice procedures agreed
* competence improved.

Moreover, the sense of having a shared voice and participation is itself beneficial. In the voluntary sector, communities are often the main infrastructure, support and benefit of participants' work. After an initial induction period, volunteers are often physically separate, unable to access formal skills or training, and may have a low sense of identity with the organization. A supportive network can offer information and advice to tackle specific problems, but is valuable simply for being the only ongoing framework within which volunteers work. In a talk in 2014, Dion Lindsay referred to a community of volunteers with an online forum whose function was 20% problem-solving and 80% providing moral support (Lindsay, 2014). Here, a measurable outcome is simply the volunteers continuing to offer their time and effort for the organization. This is not to say that voluntary communities do not need facilitation. Indeed, people usually volunteer because they want to do valuable things, not to spend time chatting online. However, unlike in the workplace, where an unengaged employee may still perform adequately in return for their salary, engagement is essential for volunteers, and can be supported from a well-managed community.

Communication in the workplace

We begin this chapter by considering how people communicate in the workplace. Although the substance of many jobs may resemble those of the last century, technology has transformed business communication. In the 1990s, the telephone, meetings and typed messages (often produced by administrative staff) were the main methods for most workers (indeed, a student at university in the early 1990s may have used e-mail, then arrived at a workplace where it was not available). The arrival of e-mail for all enabled asynchronous communication, which workers have both welcomed and berated. On the one hand, it is easy, creates a written record, and enables two parties to have a conversation at a time convenient to them. On the other, there can be frustration when e-mails are not answered, and, as the Loughborough study referenced in Chapter 3 indicates, causes stress when e-mails requiring action arrive in great volume. Actual communication can be poor, as messages are lost in overfull inboxes, or ignored by overworked staff. Moreover, as the last chapter indicates, e-mail is a poor repository for structured IM.

Many of the communications tools developed since the 1990s aim to tackle the features of e-mail, to retain the good parts and lose the less-desirable. Let us consider those features. E-mails:

* are one-to-one messages
* are asynchronous
* create a record
* are easily initiated
* can be retrieved with little effort
* have a poor structure
* show multiple threads of conversations
* create multiple copies.

The alternatives to e-mail discussed in the sections below took some of these features and used new social technology to improve them. Most of these channels developed outside the workplace, but were adopted to try and improve communication among workers. Over time, it was recognised that not just communication but collaboration and learning could be improved by using models taken from social networks. Today, many organizations offer online spaces for staff to collaborate and share information. They may be as simple as an online space for 'general discussion' or be highly curated spaces for specific groups of professionals to collaborate. They may go beyond mere discussion to host processes with targeted outcomes. The extent to which they work to improve the way that workers communicate, learn and collaborate depends very much on the organization and the needs of the relevant group.

Discussion forums

In the early years of the world wide web, content creation was considered a specialist activity, and a 'broadcast' model of communication was the norm. In the early 2000s, experts began to predict a move towards more user-generated content and interactivity, so called Web 2.0 (O'Reilly and Battelle, 2005). On the open web, this was characterised by discussion forums (an iteration of online discussion forum systems popular with early adopters of internet technology, such as Usenet newsgroups), news article comments, wikis and other collaborative platforms. This was supported by easily used blogging software, which did not require technical expertise to publish content to the web. The emergence of social media platforms such as Facebook and Twitter is consistent with the notion of the web as a conversational tool, rather than a publication platform.

Over time, it was recognised that these platforms might have a place in the workplace. Organizations with highly controlled corporate intranets saw an opportunity to give staff the means of generating informal content and sharing information. Some managers felt they could solve some of the problems of e-mail with discussion forums, at the very least reducing large numbers of e-mails backed up on servers in those days of expensive network storage. Others felt technology might solve problems created by globalised workplaces, allowing staff to communicate cheaply across continents. Forward-thinking managers recognised that using work online space to encourage discussion could be a benefit in and of itself.

Discussion forums offer the following characteristics as a communication and collaboration tool. They:

- are many to many
- have a shared history
- are all in one place
- are immediate
- are asynchronous (but publicly so – a time-lag in response is seen by everyone)
- are easy to set up and host with minimal intervention and cost
- have a limited structure in most cases (although potentially can be highly structured)

* have no guarantee that the contents will be relevant, useful, timely or important
* are not limited by organization or geography.

Euan Semple started the staff discussion forum talk.gateway at the BBC in 2000. He initially met resistance with his colleagues in internal communications: 'Some at the BBC saw his project as a waste of time and he initially had to fight to get people to accept it' (Catone, 2007). In an interview Semple described how he started it cheaply, using existing servers and put minimal staff intervention into it (Weinberger, 2005). He also allowed it to grow by word of mouth, rather than with any centralised corporate communications. Starting slowly, this very simple discussion forum gained widespread adoption by staff. It had the advantage that the BBC was at that time fostering a culture of innovation and best practice in online content. One of the authors, a former BBC employee, was a keen user in its early years and can corroborate that discussions ranged from purely professional issues ('Can anyone recommend a potential interviewee for Saturday's programme on x topic?') to work-related ('Why is the cycle parking such a mess?') to completely irrelevant ('What is the best cat food?'). There were some guidelines and occasionally obvious moderation (for example, it was technically possible to access the site using a personal e-mail, but users were supposed to identify themselves with their BBC e-mail address and discussions were removed it they did not). Although some structure had been created, most people posted in the two main areas 'General Discussions' and 'Queries and Questions'. Given its popularity, it is likely that questions asked on the forum replaced or preempted individual transactions by e-mail and telephone. Some of these questions may never have been asked by staff afraid to demonstrate their ignorance.

talk.gateway achieved its position against internal opposition through being introduced under the radar. Being seen as belonging to staff rather than as a corporate mouthpiece probably also helped adoption. On the whole users behaved well, and perhaps the insistence that posters identified themselves by their corporate e-mail account helped to encourage this. Anecdotally, some staff, both then and now, feel it is used far less by programme-makers than by staff working in online or technical support roles. Despite the high figures of adoption quoted in the articles above – '450,000 page views a month from 8,000 unique users' (Weinberger, 2005) – it developed a reputation as a forum for a clique of repeat users. Nevertheless, it started the online conversation space at the BBC and provided an outlet for staff to connect across different departments.

At the BBC, discussion forum users were on the whole confident and articulate, and organizational culture may have underlaid this. One of the authors of this book had a different experience with a SharePoint departmental discussion list in a far more conservative organization. After seeding relevant discussion topics, some staff started to engage but posts were overwhelmingly from one sector of young, high-status professional staff. Staff lower down in the hierarchy did not have the confidence to speak out, in some cases feeling that once a consensus of opinion had become evident, there was no point expressing their dissent. They also were not as confident as more senior staff that their contributions would be considered positively by their managers, either because of the content or because they were seen to be spending time away from their core tasks. Partly as a result of these problems, this discussion forum was never widely adopted. In other organizations we have seen senior staff happy to use social tools within their own peer group, but setting permissions to exclude others in the organization.

These scenarios are probably rarer than they once were. Most global organizations are accustomed to staff using internal and external forums to communicate and find information, and would not penalise them for doing so. In many organizations the culture is now far more autonomous than previously, reflecting the fact that managers are often absent, colleagues remote and workers far less likely to be measured on their behaviour than on their measured outputs. Unless there is a disciplinary situation, it is unlikely that managers have the time or inclination to check users' online behaviour. In fact, in some organizations, the number and quality of contributions on internal discussion forums are considered to be part of users' performance. The number of posts marked by a user's peers as useful becomes part of their profile. Participation may even be measured as part of performance review.

You may still encounter resistance to open discussion forums, particularly if your organization is in the public sector, or anywhere where the public behaviour of staff is likely to come under scrutiny. More old-fashioned organizations may still consider their use a distraction from core tasks, particularly for those lower in the hierarchy. But, at the time of writing, most organizations do not have to fight in the same way to achieve recognition that informal discussion online can be a valuable way of sharing knowledge, and make it accessible to a larger group than one-to-one communication like e-mails.

Bulletin-board style discussion forums are not the only options for informal organizational social media. These are some popular tools currently in use:

* *Jive* allows forums for posting questions among groups and rewards

participation through gamification (badges and points). Users have profiles and can be alerted about relevant discussion threads through mentions.

* *Yammer* is another business social media platform, often described as 'Facebook for business'. It allows users to share content and build and join networks and social feeds.
* *Slack* is an enormously popular discussion application used particularly in technical communities. With a light-touch distribution of permissions, it allows workers to congregate around different discussion topics and collaborate on documents. Its layout and set-up make it easy to use but it is notably weak as a source of stored information.
* *Google Hangouts* allow threaded discussion topics to be initiated within a permissions structure, which can be tailored to the needs of an individual organization. Google Hangouts can be used by organizations which have implemented G Suite as their corporate platform.
* *Microsoft Teams* is Microsoft's answer to Slack on the Office 365 platform. The platform creates spaces for groups to collaborate on different 'channels' (Slack terminology) and share documents.
* *Social learning platforms* such as Docebo started as organizational iterations of course management software such as Moodle and Blackboard (which has its own business iteration). They are used in much the same way as the others in this list, as places to have conversations, collaborate on documents and share information.

Tools like this are key in the battle against e-mail. One of the authors worked for a global financial services firm which introduced Slack to its developer teams. The firm implemented different peer groups, matching the developers' interests and concerns. Permission structures were set fairly loosely, which encouraged engagement, although the knowledge manager was able to moderate and intervene when thought helpful. The roll-out was supported with training during which users were asked to think before they sent communications. After Slack was introduced, the flow of e-mails reduced and more conversation took place in a central place which everyone could access. The ease of chat reduced ephemeral conversations from users' inboxes and created a single focal point for different groups' collaborative efforts. This is an example of where an easy-to-use tool can engage users with just enough control to mitigate risks.

Communities of practice

Online communities of practice use similar technology to discussion forums, but usually involve more thought and planning and are focused around specific professional groups. Their online iteration may, in fact, only be a small part of their function. They aim to bring professionals with a shared set of concerns into discussion in a way that helps everyone to learn from each other, collaborate and share knowledge. Many communities of practice exist across different organizations and flourish informally and formally, using social media channels, e-mail discussion lists or 'walled gardens' such as locked-down team sites. In many cases formal membership is unnecessary, participation is voluntary, and growth and decline organic. Communities of practice are valuable in helping people feel comfortable as they go about their work, regardless of whether or not they are interacting over work-related issues, though as a knowledge manager, you are most likely to be facilitating communities centred around professional issues.

Online communities offer great advantages as communications spaces. Like discussion forums they are instant and have a history, but have an inbuilt structure that make them useful repositories for knowledge about a particular subject. The next chapter considers aspects of how far governance and curation can enhance the informational value of an online space (potentially at the expense of spontaneity), but even a light-touch online community provides a retrospective space where knowledge can be mined at a later date. In summary, online communities:

* offer many-to-many communications
* have a single location
* have a shared history
* are immediate
* are asynchronous
* need some governance, rules and set-up procedures
* are structured around shared topics, can be highly structured and linked to related topics
* have varied, potentially useful, content posted by engaged members of staff,

As mentioned, communities of practice exist regardless of any online iteration. Etienne Wenger's extensive anthropological work in organizations, in particular his book *Communities of Practice* (1998), was groundbreaking in its day in helping people to understand how workers learn through identity and collaboration. He describes practices that develop in working life as 'collective

Case study 4.1: Managing your online communities

Organization B is a professional advisory firm whose KIM team decided to set up online communities of practice as part of a SharePoint implementation. Although not the primary reason for the implementation, the option of setting up online spaces for different communities within the organization was seen as an additional benefit and there had been some call from particular groups for online space where they could collaborate.

When initially set up, a light-touch system of governance was laid out. A set of guidelines was produced outlining what constituted appropriate online behaviour. The team within IT which managed the system had some rough criteria as to when to approve a site and could refer borderline cases to the KM department. Staff who requested sites with particular features such as discussion forums could be refused. For example, only time-limited communities, such as those around projects, were allowed to host document repositories within the site, to avoid document proliferation (the assumption being that a full review would take place at the end of the project, and documents moved to a suitable repository). Although the KM department had some responsibilities around moderation, or at least referring behaviour to line managers, it was generally expected that most site requests of staff above a certain level would be fulfilled.

The first sites were set up for pilot users who were involved in the platform implementation and development of governance. They had a clear understanding of what they wanted to achieve and helped to lay the boundaries of what the sites should be for. Their sites were generally well used by small groups and were closed down when they were no longer needed. Ironically governance around appropriate behaviour proved largely unnecessary. Staff understood that they were at work while online, and moderated their activity accordingly. More important was the need to ensure that users understood what sites were for and were only issued with them if they could make use of them.

Over time, more people within the organization started to request sites. Although KM staff were empowered to refuse, or suggest that users join a similar existing community, generally speaking nobody was refused a site, partly because of an inbuilt culture of deference, and partly because it was felt that too many barriers would prevent staff enjoying the full benefits of the platform. This resulted in site sprawl, as sites developed with few active users and little ongoing engagement. No clear governance was in place as to when a site should be closed down. Eventually hundreds of sites existed of which very few were genuinely active, although there were some clear successes. These were generally where an emerging or existing community needed to tackle communication problems. The remainder were underused and contained very little of value.

The knowledge team took the opportunity of a move to a new intranet and KM platform to close down the former community of practice collection. Each site owner was contacted and had to make a case for migrating the community to the new system. Additionally, the team established firmer rules as to why the site was needed, and could approve all new sites. This was done in connection with implementing an informal discussion space (which had not existed before). The existence of this space, which any staff member could access in order to engage in discussion, made it possible to place far stricter rules around the new community of practice collection. As there was a culture of deference, which had not changed significantly, some underused sites were migrated at the request of senior staff, and duplication of sites remained where senior users were unwilling to join another community. However, overall, there were far fewer sites and those which survived were better used, supporting more engagement with a wider range of staff.

learning', suggesting that as groups of people work together, they align their practices and learn from each other. He points out that while we are constantly exposed to new information, we select what we choose to add to our body of knowledge. Being in a community of practice allows us to process information at the correct level we need to carry out our work. These practices are the shared 'property' of members of the same community. He points to the fact that being part of this community not only helps staff do their jobs better, but also increases the quantity of job satisfaction they experience. How they do this is not always expressed in written form, but his characterisation does not distinguish between tacit and explicit knowledge. In fact it is his thesis that the two constantly work together, as communities of practice produce new information artefacts (explicitly) and (tacitly) find new ways of creating meaning from them.

To some extent, everyone in the workplace is in a community of practice, whether defined or not. Wenger describes practice as 'a process by which we can experience the world and our engagement with it as meaningful' (1998, 51). We use our social interactions in the workplace as a means of making sense of the work we do, providing shortcuts in language and inference. Communities of practice also fill the gaps provided by imperfect processes and systems (and as we pointed out in Chapter 3, these are inevitable). Wenger describes how organizational software theoretically led the worker through processes necessary to get their job done (1998, 46). In reality, workers consulted colleagues, searched for more information, and generally found ways of reconciling the constrictions of the system they used with the reality of the information they needed. Communities of practice can thus be considered to fill in the gaps that corporate systems present us with.

Communities of practice reflect the changes and mitigate the limitations of the modern workplace. Staff are less likely now to be working in large teams with colleagues carrying out similar work and more likely to be the only person who does what they do. In this context, reaching across their organization provides support they may not get from their own team. Their peers may be in other offices, cities or countries, or may even be outside their organization. Additionally, many organizations have a far weaker infrastructure than they once did, relying on online self-service rather than support departments like HR. Managers often have far less time for hands-on staff management. In these situations, online communities provide the missing support which enables workers to go about their jobs.

Communities of practice also have a role to play as organizations become leaner and smaller. In the past 20 years they have been an effective tool in the third sector, to support volunteers, provide identity and engagement, and an infrastructure not otherwise available to them. As many services become outsourced to the voluntary sector, service providers may find themselves participating in or facilitating such communities. It may be a challenge to encourage internal workers and voluntary staff to work together if the latter have seen colleagues leave because of downsizing or redundancy. Paid staff may resent passing on their knowledge to volunteers and the facilitation model common in charities may feel alien to them. More benignly, professional communities of practice may develop by practitioners in different organizations, whether formally, led by representative organizations, or informally across a range of public social media platforms. Schopflin (2017) discussed the different forms this might take.

Wenger wrote about communities of practice agnostic of any platform created for them. As a knowledge manager, you are likely to be involved in curating communities of practice in an online space. But it is important to remember that they already exist in your organization and may have been functioning well for decades. You therefore need to consider what you can offer. Wenger makes clear that communities of practice offer value by helping workers negotiate their way through the tasks they have to achieve, and they do this whether or not discussions are specifically about work-related matters. Yet as a community facilitator you are likely to be setting up, curating or moderating communities in a more or less formalised work-related context. Where Wenger wrote about a relatively informal group of low-paid workers, communities of practice can favour groups with a formal identity and status.

The advantage of a considered and supported community of practice is that it can find a form which exactly meets the needs of a group of users. Communities of practice need differing levels of specificity. The larger and more heterogeneous the group, the less specific its language, topics and engagements. This type of community may include a wider range of people, but offer less relevant value to participants. Smaller groups, with a shared outlook and language, can support tools such as taxonomies which make expressed knowledge easier to contain. But small communities of practice can be very demanding of knowledge manager time, and reinforce existing organizational hierarchies. The amount of effort you put into supporting smaller communities should reflect the value you think their knowledge-sharing will bring to the organization as a whole.

Before we look at what we think makes a community of practice work, we would like to briefly outline some variant forms. In the rest of this chapter we generally refer to communities of practice but our observations also apply to communities of interest, communities of purpose and the champions model.

Communities of interest

While communities of practice are populated by practitioners in a particular area of work, communities of interest can be formed around any topic. Their members share an identity which is often nothing to do with work, but can operate within the workplace, providing a space for workers to bond on shared topics of interest. Examples are groups formed around books, knitting or football. Communities of interest can be work-related, for example, a group following technical or industry developments, or workplace-related, for example, a group of people who cycle to work. They are also a way of connecting people at similar places in their career who work in different practice areas. In the workplaces which support them, they are often formed spontaneously, engaging members from the start. Communities of interest can be powerful places, which achieve solid results through focused work, where communities of practice remain talking shops.

Communities of interest are generally positive places and worth encouraging regardless of any expected return on investment. When encouraged properly, they enable users facing similar fears and challenges to share experiences. They are particularly helpful for global organizations, whose workers often struggle to adjust to working with managers and colleagues they have never met, or who regularly move as part of their work. Users can connect over more than just work issues and can share tips on all sorts of subjects, for example, moving to new countries. Some organizations encourage first time managers to use communities of interest to connect with similar peer groups and share experiences. A community of interest can be a safe place to ask questions from 'How do I approve annual leave?' to 'Do I allow staff more than two weeks' leave at any time?' Communities of interest allow users to build their own networks and social groups and to transfer knowledge seamlessly.

Communities of purpose

Communities of purpose have a specific, probably time-limited goal. Although the goals might not be officially termed projects, or the communities be following any project-related methodology, they come together for a specific outcome and use both physical and online spaces to achieve them. They are usually relatively unproblematic as they have a clear idea of what they want to achieve. The KM role may be largely to provide online spaces and other tools to help participants share what they need to in a timely fashion. While their operation may be fairly informal, having a close-down date can work as a focal point to review successes and failures. They are therefore an area where informal communication could result in a legacy.

Staff involved in current projects can improve their practice by sharing not simply within their own community of purpose, but also between projects. A community of practice between project managers can be a good way for otherwise discrete groups to learn from each other's mistakes and successes, and share 'tools, templates and examples' (Trees, 2017b). It should also enable those involved in expensive and resource-intensive projects to work more closely in alignment, beyond the traditional assumptions and contingencies of traditional project paperwork.

This type of sharing requires a healthy culture. If projects are competing for resources and executive attention, participants are not motivated to take time to share with other teams. However, they are an excellent means of tackling the inward-looking nature of project teams, who rarely get an opportunity to see their work with fresh eyes. Where projects occur within particular practice areas within an organization, it can be helpful for them to share a community of practice space across projects – a balance between the detailed community of purpose the project itself has, and the generalised sharing across different corporate projects.

The champions model

The champions model is a community centred around an activity which is not part of a worker's defined job, but an additional responsibility shared with others in the organization. Examples are records management or intranet champions, where members combine their knowledge of, and influence within, their own department with a set of values or practices developed outside. Case study 4.2 opposite shows how this model can work by giving members a sense of ownership and reward above and beyond their day job, providing identity and job satisfaction. It is worth remembering that champions are not always the

Case study 4.2: Building a champions network

Organization A is a large technology sales company, whose managers used the opportunity presented by a new intranet deployment to introduce the idea of a social intranet to the organization. As well as providing standard edited intranet content, the aim was to introduce blogging, microblogging, and the ability to share content, like, rate and comment. Senior staff were highly engaged with this vision and wanted to ensure that adoption would be organization-wide. In order to drive change a network of content champions was set up, to encourage early adoption, train colleagues on the system and lead by example. The champions carried out their work in addition to their day job and had no financial reward.

Careful thought was put into getting the best out of this champions group and ensuring that they understood their role and its importance, and were engaged in the change process from start to finish. They needed to understand that the project had the tools to deliver the expected changes and that they were empowered to help it.

These were the main factors behind the success of this network's operation:

- Staff members needed to volunteer to be champions: there was no point in coercing unwilling colleagues as it was unlikely there would be any change if they were not enthusiastic.
- Champions were engaged with the project from the start, participating in user acceptance testing and in workshops as the requirements for the system were being identified. This built a strong sense of inclusion.
- Champions were asked informally to agree to a set of terms of conditions and ensure that their managers were happy for them to dedicate work time to the role. Given the senior and executive support for the project, there was relatively little resistance from managers.
- This high-profile support meant that staff understood that everyone would be using the new intranet, so having an early adopter on their team could be an advantage.
- Any member of staff could be a champion and there was no job description, so the network represented a very good cross section of the organization (though weighted towards staff from support services such as IT and HR rather than frontline staff such as those working in sales).
- Champions benefited from receiving training on the system and in soft skills relating to communications, KM and user engagement, as well as having their profile raised within the organization.
- Champions had early access and the opportunity to provide feedback and hence shape the system. The project team listened to this feedback and acted on it, fixing early glitches and showing that they valued the champions' opinion.
- Before carrying out any advocacy work, they were provided with training, the tools they needed, materials and each other's support. They were given train-the-trainer sessions, access to the system weeks before it went live, and resources such as slide decks animations and infographics.
- Champions and early adopters were given targets and goals and attempts were made at gamification. Some were even set 'homework' to write blog posts. This

fitted in with the organization's culture where support and positivity were rewarded and success was celebrated.

Groups of champions were asked to run open days, training staff and giving demonstrations before the intranet launch. Every major office around the globe was able to run at least one training or drop-in session, and most did several, both before and immediately after the launch. As part of the champion engagement programme, champions were encouraged to use the new social tools and share content with colleagues, to show them what the new technology could do, and how they could be part of it. This continued after the initial launch and they are encouraged to hold quarterly open days and drop-in sessions in their own offices to ensure that support and engagement continues. Some have continued to be system experts, engaging directly with the vendors.

As a result, there was widespread interaction with the new social tools from the launch date. Instead of being invested in a small project team, expertise was spread throughout the organization. Participation dropped off after the launch and recruiting new champions when others left was difficult without the buzz and build up of an approaching launch date. However, formal and informal channels were maintained to keep the sense of community, notably discussion forums and online chats.

This was a project involving significant cultural change. The company had not previously experimented with organizational social tools for communication or knowledge-sharing. The technology itself was not as good as it could have been, which damaged adoption and credibility. Notably, the microblogging technology did not work in the same way as Twitter, the microblogging tool most likely to have been used by staff in their personal lives. However, there was an increase in engagement of over 65% on the previous intranet system. While not an unequivocal success, there is no doubt that a well-managed champions network was key to this particular community of purpose.

most influential people in their work teams, and are often not measured or rewarded for this work. They therefore require considerable support. A knowledge manager may struggle to gain engagement if their line manager is antagonistic, or their identity is more closely tied up with their day job.

Supporting successful communities

As facilitator of communities, your work will be in three main areas:

* building the community
* facilitating communication
* making a record of output.

As we have stated, you may be required to produce some tangible output in order to demonstrate that your community is successful, but the most valuable part of your work is in building the community and facilitating communication. Anecdotally, users are thought to prefer to ask questions anew rather than search existing records of discussion, so the legacy is ultimately less important than facilitating communication between people to help them share knowledge. Chapter 5 looks in more detail at means of capturing knowledge for reuse.

We would like to stress that there is no single best way to approach communities of practice. Some communities act as a reference or problem-solving forum. Others may simply appear to be a talking shop, but these too can be valuable. Never underestimate the tacit knowledge exchange which takes place once employees have a space where they feel free to engage in discussion. Even the knowledge that they are part of a community which understands the problems they face daily can be a source of confidence and strength. Supportive communities can prevent high staff turnover and ensure that knowledge and expertise stay within the organization.

Building the community

As previously mentioned, there may already be thriving communities within your organization. For these, you can focus on facilitating the community. Case study 4.1 demonstrates that you may be in a position where you need to build a community from scratch, whether – as in this case – because of a new corporate venture, or because the support of a community is needed to tackle a lack of knowledge-sharing or moral support among a group of workers. Here are some suggestions which may help build your community:

* *Start with face to face*: early studies of community of practice, such as the Xerox agents in Seely Brown and Duguid's study (2000), were largely physical and formed organically. To achieve the same level of engagement in a virtual forum can be difficult without at least some face-to-face contact.
* *Find pioneers*: staff working in knowledge-rich areas operating successfully often have little motivation to participate with others outside their existing communication channels and may feel that using internal social networking tools only reveals that they are not busy enough. To win them over, you can start by co-opting a trusted member of their community who can demonstrate the benefits of sharing knowledge.
* *Start in stages*: some communities may only feel safe sharing knowledge in a walled garden. This is less than ideal, but better than no knowledge-sharing at all.

* *Offer reward*: gamification is sometimes used to encourage people to participate in online communities by offering rewards for the most posts, especially in technical and professional services firms. This is not a sustainable approach, but helps populate an empty space and may encourage long-term adoption.
* *Give a sense of autonomy*: you need to show participants that they own the space and are at no risk of censure from sharing. Most KIM practices benefit from management adoption and leadership. Communities work better if managers stay away.
* *Embed in organizational practice*: conversely, it is important that managers understand the value of communities of practices and support staff engagement. You may find them more supportive once you have already built a successful community of practice or may be lucky to find a pioneer. Such managers may even introduce involvement in the community of practice into staff performance review. This is helpful to engagement as long as it does not feel like a box-ticking exercise to the employee ('Have I had my five interactions this month?').

Facilitating the community

Here are some suggestions which may help facilitate your community:

* *Tackle problems which really exist with tools that help*: one of the authors of this book worked with an established physically disparate department that already worked well as a community owing to good leadership and regularly timetabled meetings. However there was no space for communication while apart. Case study 5.1 in the next chapter outlines how this problem was tackled.
* *Be flexible*: not every team wants structure in their forum, but some do. Some may benefit from a full-scale taxonomy, surfacing relevant content from other areas in the organization. Others may just want a space to post links and make contact.
* *Seed content*: nobody asks questions on an unused forum. As well as posting relevant content yourself, use your pioneer contacts to get things going.
* *Moderate and facilitate*: you can help maintain credibility in an online space by stepping in where questions are left unanswered or a discussion is moving in an unhelpful direction. You can even offer help where appropriate. One of the authors monitored problems shared on online

forums and stepped in where appropriate to offer a better technical solution (such as a conference call) where he thought it would help. He also directed users to previous threads on the same topic and other groups that might help.

* *Don't govern too much*: if an online community is providing value, even if not in the way intended, then let it continue. If it is working without your input then let the members of the community feel they own it themselves.
* *Keep engagement going*: has a community gone quiet? It may be that engagement has moved to another area, or that it was in fact really based around a very few people who have moved on. If you feel its members would still benefit from the community, investigate what is needed to re-engage them.
* *Close unused forums down*: let users know and direct them to new spaces if appropriate, but there is no point in maintaining communities of practice that don't function as online communities. Perhaps there was never really a community of practice. Or perhaps it works perfectly well in a context outside your control.

Recording output

As is probably clear, we think that as much value comes from the community role in supporting identity as from tangible outputs. However, and this is particularly true in communities of purpose, tangible outputs can be used as a means of building a shared record. Here are some examples of where this can work:

* *Mine your forums for intranet content*: questions which recur regularly can help make content on your authoritative sources of information more relevant and helpful. They also provide a refresher on the terms and contexts in which people are seeking information.
* *Examine metrics*: how often communities are used and in what ways may provide a health warning for different communities. You can track drop-offs in engagement to the health or otherwise of a particular activity and address it as appropriate.
* *Keep track of informal discussions to gain a sense of hot topics*: regular questions on an industry issue might suggest there is a need for a more formal knowledge repository on the issue.
* *Offer help in archiving content*: if a discussion or online community of practice has produced a useful record which should have a legacy, you can step in and find a home for it somewhere it can easily be found by staff.

Informal knowledge-sharing is immediate and accessible and can be the easiest means of getting staff to share. Content produced may or may not be considered authoritative, and this may or may not matter to your organization.

Recommended approaches

Social technologies in the workplace offer opportunities for increased knowledge-sharing. A key function for knowledge managers has been building and co-ordinating online sharing tools, and otherwise supporting communities to share across temporal, physical and organizational boundaries. Ways of meeting the challenges of engaging staff vary, depending on your organization and the community you are working with, but you can use online and physical forums to solve problems, provide identity and support, and facilitate informal discussion. As will be clear from this chapter, we believe that this work is valuable in and of itself, regardless of any measured outcomes. This is not to say that this type of knowledge-sharing never offers a legacy. Indeed, it can form the basis for the type of knowledge capture we cover in the next chapter. This and the next chapter can be seen as overlapping ends of a spectrum, with bulletin-board or microblogging-style ephemera at one end and locked-down authoritative content at the other.

What to consider when managing online communities
Permissions
Most platforms support a permissions structure allowing different users to post, set up new discussion areas and moderate. Some communities allow frequent posters, or those marked highly by other users, more privileges. How much governance you impose on permissions may depend on other factors, such as the ability to post anonymously, or your corporate culture. However, the looser your permissions structure, the more engagement you are likely to gain and the more diverse the voices you will recruit. Ideally users should not need any further logins to connect with your community: A single sign-in should designate permissions automatically.

Structure
The more structure, the more useful an online community is to others and the better its legacy. However, putting in barriers such as the need to choose a subject area is likely to minimise engagement. As a moderator or facilitator, you can pre-set categories for discussion, but you may find users continue to post in a single area. An online community already focused around a shared interest offers an inbuilt structure. Members' shared outlook and language may also make structure and categorisation within the community easier than a general discussion forum.

Engagement

As the above suggests, the fewer barriers you put in place, the more likely users are to add content to your online communities. Engagement is probably easier now than it once was, depending on your corporate culture, as users are more accustomed to entering public debate in an online workspace. However, you may still need to seed content to demonstrate the value of your space. If you manage a specific community of practice, you can engage members offline. Ideally you should involve them from the start and encourage them to make their online space in their own image.

Location look and feel

Do you want your community to be seen as part of the intranet, or as a separate, interactive space? Will the platform be open to all, or restricted to specific communities? How your users navigate to online communities, and what they see when they reach them, will help shape their experience and understanding of what they see.

Measurement

Although we believe online communities are an excellent tool, which should not need justifying, you may need to demonstrate value with some metrics. Numbers, frequency and diversity of interactions are all useful ways of assessing them, and can also help you fine-tune other aspects of the online space. Gamification – awarding prizes for numbers of interactions – may increase the number of interactions, but it has the danger that it may be merely a box-ticking exercise and not show sustainable engagement.

Further reading

Lindsay, D. (2014) Communities of Practice for the Post Recession Environment, NetIKX event, 16 September, https://netikx.wordpress.com/2014/09/22/communities-of-practice-for-the-post-recession-environment-tuesday-16th-september-2014/ [accessed 25 March 2018].

Seely Brown, J. and Duguid, P. (2000) *The Social Life of Information*, Harvard Business School Press.

Wenger, E. (1998) *Communities of Practice: learning, meaning, and identity*, Cambridge University Press.

Chapter 5

Making knowledge explicit: knowledge bases, know-how and wikis

This chapter is about the structured homes we make for expressed knowledge: wikis, enquiries databases, frequently asked questions (FAQs), knowledge bases and know-how pages. Such expressions of shared learning have always existed in organizations, either as official, final, published documents or as quality-assured databases managed by professionals. They were reliable and authoritative, but a coagulation of knowledge at a particular moment. Modern tools allow knowledge repositories to be continually updated and represent a wide range of voices. However, all such repositories are compromises between authority and immediacy, and certain, approved knowledge and ongoing thoughts and opinions under discussion. They are also compromises between the diversity of views held by participants and a consensus turned into accepted fact. Structure, provided by categories and tags, offers a means of helping users find information in the future, but can be burdensome for contributors to add as they contribute. And any structure is itself a compromise as subject tags always are, whether imposed by a KIM professional, worked out within a group, or referring to an already existing corporate or industry taxonomy.

Many people writing about KM like to suggest that, once recorded, knowledge becomes information. In his highly amusing take-down of the then emerging fad of KM, Wilson (2002) asserted that knowledge 'cannot be 'captured' – it can only be demonstrated through our expressible knowledge and through our acts'. Wilson was working within a framework which suggested that knowledge acquisition is something that happens as we negotiate our way through the world. The artefacts we create along the way relate to this knowledge, but are not knowledge themselves. Wenger (1998) felt that the 'reifications' of ongoing learning and knowledge-sharing (such as databases, manuals or reports) are valuable even though they could only ever be temporary and imperfect representations of an ongoing practice. Whatever you call these reified objects, and whether or not you consider them to be knowledge or merely information, they are an essential part of the corporate record. A huge and essential part of the work of the knowledge manager is to facilitate the creation of repositories of corporate knowledge and to manage them in such a way that content can be found again.

Knowledge repositories are among the most visible means of showing KIM in action. Organizations are often motivated to introduce a KM programme to gain more benefit from existing internal knowledge. Thus, the creation of an explicit knowledge repository is often the first KM initiative in a new corporate programme. A full and flourishing repository can be shown to management teams and demonstrates that corporate knowledge can be tamed, and captured. But this is not necessarily the best approach to making knowledge explicit. Creating a repository does not mean it will actually be used. Can engagement by adding content be equated with use of that content? How often do people simply just ask the same questions again, rather than search knowledge bases? And how do you prove a knowledge repository's existence has helped the organization flourish and meet its goals?

Another issue to approach when managing knowledge repositories is how far to exert authority and intervene editorially. As with the knowledge communities explored in the previous chapter, you will find yourself creating a balance between engagement and control. If users add to a repository frequently it will contain a treasury of organizational intellectual capital, but how reliable is it? If it could change from one day to the next, can you point people towards the knowledge within it? By contrast, a highly curated wiki or knowledge base will be authoritative and grow in value, capturing staff expertise as it is exercised, and transforming it into an encyclopedia-type resource. But such a repository will be resource-intensive. You need to train colleagues and persuade them to contribute and are likely to spend a lot of your own time structuring it and maintaining it. Some organizations deal with this by having both an 'unofficial' space where discussion takes place and instant knowledge is recorded, and a separate space for curated 'permanent' knowledge. Moreover, KIM initiatives like the corporate encyclopedia described in Chapter 1 can operate as beacons for KIM activity and, if run primarily by the KIM team themselves, be highly achievable within a short time frame.

Our first recommendation for knowledge repositories is to resist trying to put everything in one place, at least in large organizations. Groups with similar language and needs are more likely to share and engage in the same way, and the more centralised a repository, the less useful it is for all members. Having said this, one of the less recognised benefits of corporate KM is enabling a range of voices to be heard, and to allow those at the front line in organizations to access specialist knowledge. So it is worth encouraging spaces which everyone feels free to share, and small organizations without a hierarchical culture can work extremely well on a single corporate platform. But, as the last chapter suggested, smaller groups may hide in their own spaces if they feel an organization-wide platform does not suit them.

A second piece of advice for anyone implementing a structured knowledge base is to consult users. You may be asked to set up knowledge sites by a senior person, but make sure you find out what types of resource would benefit actual users. What are their problems, and how could a knowledge repository solve them? What type of journey are they going to make to find the knowledge they need? What language resonates with them? Knowledge bases are far too often creator-led and it is a danger that information professionals in particular fall into, to curate a set of consistent, controlled spaces that users find intimidating and do not actually use. Knowledge repositories strongly led by subject matter experts also fall into this trap. The latter may intimidate the knowledge manager into using a structure which reflects how their profession ought to work, but not how it does in practice. Information should be structured to mirror the way it will be assimilated by users. We strongly recommend carrying out user experience testing, developing personas and understanding the information-seeking behaviours of your users. Use your findings as your basis for building knowledge repositories, not an externally mandated structure.

We also recommend taking an agnostic approach to technology until you have identified user knowledge needs. This is true of all KM and IM approaches, but it feels worth stressing it here, because knowledge repositories can be time- and effort-intensive to produce, so it is important to get your approach right. Too often organizations are led by the technology available to them and build knowledge platforms because they can, rather than to meet an understood need. You should have a clearly defined strategy based on specific issues which need addressing. Finally, this strategy should underlie a sustainable approach. Knowledge bases are often implemented as part of a single project. Who is going to update them and do those persons understand what that means? What is in it for them and how do you ensure the knowledge base is of wider benefit?

In short, do not simply build a knowledge repository because it is nice to have. Find out your users' needs and develop something that will meet them.

Knowledge organizing systems

As a knowledge manager, you may be asked to build or apply a taxonomy or knowledge organization system. Loosely defined, a taxonomy is a set of category labels which can be applied to information objects so that things similar to each other can be found in the same place, or from the same search, regardless of how they are described. Taxonomies are associated with traditional classification and indexing systems, with web and intranet navigations and with records management file plans. In these cases, they are usually at least to some extent used to classify an already existing body of knowledge. In KIM systems, users can add categories as they create content. As the sidebar indicates, employees add to corporate knowledge bases either by putting consent in a location already identified as having certain taxonomical properties (such as subject matter or content type) or by adding a label. So, if I want to share an article about a type of technology, I can either choose a location already containing content on this topic, or I can post anywhere I like and add a relevant subject label, ideally from a prepared list. In the latter case, you can then create pages which automatically bring to the surface all content tagged with the same term, or use it to make search results more relevant.

The key challenge of knowledge taxonomies is that you cannot expect users to be skilled or even comfortable with classification. Mandating the addition of a subject term will make your knowledge store more useful, but discourage some users from participating. Additionally, classification terms are always a compromise of mutually understood language, because individuals are likely instinctively to prefer different terms to describe similar concepts. Some may also not really understand the purpose of classifying content and choose the simplest term available (in a tax accountant firm, for example, choosing 'taxation' for everything posted). The more closely aligned the user group is to the concepts they are discussing and the language they use to describe them, the better its members will understand the categories and apply them correctly. As case study 5.1 shows, they may still need a helping hand to begin with, but should be able to understand how the taxonomy works on their own eventually.

There are several approaches to classification. Consider a news article about security issues using blockchain technology as a basis for cryptocurrency (a popular topic at the time of writing). It has a number of properties (called 'facets' in classification terminology) such as content type (news, rather than an internal paper or academic journal article), when it was posted, country of origin and topic. The topic could be assigned a range of different labels depending on who

Case study 5.1: Using your users' language

A membership organization had a field-based sales team who worked in different sectors and different parts of the country. It was recognised that their disparate nature was potentially damaging, as trends in members' needs could be internalised by a single salesperson but not shared with others. The sales team had a supportive culture, backed up by frequent calls and monthly meetings, and experience was valued, reflected in the long service that some team members had built up. Crucially, although each salesperson had an individual target, it was team targets – based around the different membership sectors – which were most closely examined as measures of success. This encouraged peer mentoring and knowledge-sharing, within the barriers of physical separation.

To support knowledge-sharing, a target was introduced that each month every team member must e-mail three pieces of new sector intelligence to the sectoral sales lead. If they did not fulfil this, they would not receive their bonus, no matter how good their sales performance had been. However, the process was not highly valued by team members. Once they e-mailed their intelligence, it was collated and edited by sales leads, who submitted it to the head of sales, who then combined it into a single document, which was circulated in time for their monthly sales meeting. An additional sign-off was also needed from the marketing department. By the time it was discussed, staff felt that intelligence came too late to help them, although they recognised it was of use to the company as a whole. Therefore they tended to see their contributions as a box-ticking exercise rather than something genuinely beneficial to them. And nobody ever submitted more than three pieces of intelligence.

In an attempt to assist them, the knowledge manager set up a SharePoint list to which they could add new information immediately after site visits (and, once their devices and available Wi-Fi had improved, actually during the site visits). The list was structured around the company's different sales sectors with location as an optional category (not all intelligence came from site visits). There were optional categories based on headings agreed between the knowledge manager and sales staff, but most of the content was free text within the sectoral and geographical limits. The knowledge manager had engaged certain sales staff at an early stage to encourage their input so when the site was demonstrated, it already had some content on it, one piece of which was – at her own confession – news to the head of sales. After this more staff began to engage with the SharePoint list and after three months the previous system was abandoned.

The chief barriers to adopting the new system were technical and cultural. Technically, staff were not yet equipped to add content while out on sales visits. Some were also uncomfortable with using their laptop while in a meeting, as they were accustomed to a conversational sales style. As a result, adding content remained an administrative task, rather than one that was embedded into sales practice. This did improve once staff were issued with lighter laptops or tablets and had better access to Wi-Fi. Culturally, the chief barrier was senior staff in marketing, who were reluctant to allow sales staff to record their impressions without editorial intervention and were concerned that incorrect facts or unsanctioned opinion would be added to the list. Standards of written English were not at publication level, but sales staff did not abuse the list and the notes they made were polite and professional.

The knowledge manager initially found she was frequently editing the category list and sometimes retrospectively categorising content. However, once it became possible to show content filtered by category (and those categories had become more diverse and relevant to the issues of concern to the staff) more sales personnel began to tag content with categories themselves. As staff became able to filter a list of market intelligence by subject, sector or geographical region, they began to contribute not to achieve a monthly target, but as part of a desire to improve the content of the knowledge base. It had proven to be a valuable source of knowledge.

The success of these pages was in a large part due to the knowledge manager engaging with the team, identifying a problem, and finding a solution. Had the existing system worked for them, they would have been unlikely to change their method of sharing knowledge. It was also essential that she recruited members of the team to add content at the development stage. By demonstrating a list which was already part populated by their peers, users could see how it could work if they added content too.

is accessing it and for what purpose. Is it about money, types of technology or information security? The answer to this depends entirely on how people are likely to search for it and the level of detail they need. If users post many articles about technology, you may already have a category called 'blockchain'. When planning your taxonomical approach, you need to think of the types of content people are likely to post and offer them categorisation choices which make sense to them.

For these reasons, we suggest that taxonomies are best used in two scenarios:

- designed for specific groups likely to create a significant body of valuable content, which they will return to and use again; these groups should share a language and a level of understanding about the topic
- in a far simpler category list which can be used across corporate content; it needs to be simple enough that anyone likely to be adding content can understand it, but is only worth using if content can subsequently be found easily in a comprehensive way.

A third option is to give classification work to a KIM professional as part of their regular upkeep of a knowledge repository, so they do not just create category locations but also reactively correct or tag content with consistent metadata. Internal content tagged with a particular taxonomy term can be found in locations the content creator may not know about. I may have uploaded my article about the blockchain in a discussion list called 'Tech news'. The knowledge manager has added tags for 'information security' and 'currencies' knowing there are knowledge base pages templated to pick up any content posted with these terms. The uses for automatically surfacing content are broad. One of the authors of this book worked with an HR system which identified every staff member with particular affiliations and interests. Content was sent automatically to their newsfeed when given a relevant tag. We think this is a particularly good way of demonstrating the value of having a skilled taxonomist working behind the scenes as it allows staff to structure the knowledge they share without having to think about it themselves. In the afterword to this book, we discuss how machine learning can be applied in this context.

An essential guide for anyone building taxonomies for knowledge repositories is Helen Lippell's chapter 'Building a Corporate Taxonomy' (Lippell, 2014). She outlines the essential stages of working with colleagues to identify how they structure and label information and considers how taxonomies work to help users find and sort information, rather than act as a barrier.

Types of taxonomies in knowledge and information management

Intranet navigation

Intranets offer staff the answers to the questions they need in the course of their work. A good navigation allows staff to find information quickly under the headings they expect. Taxonomists therefore need to consider how users ask questions, what the location of the answers should be and how that location should be described.

Search taxonomies

Any body of online knowledge can use a taxonomy with its search tool, enabling a search for 'holiday' to find content labelled 'leave', 'annual leave' and other variations. The taxonomist can use existing search logs and user interviews to identify the language likely to be used, and group together terms which refer to the same thing.

Category locations

With this approach you ask the user to choose the best place to locate the content as they create it. This works best where there are a few, obvious categories. Be warned that users want to post content where they think other people will read it, so are likely to choose a popular category over a relevant one.

Templates

If you offer the opportunity for staff to create knowledge bases, team sites or even team drives, it is usual to offer a range of templates for the type of content they expect to populate the online space. It may be appropriate for different templates to already come with subject metadata, or you may ask users to choose a category before the space is set up. This enables content tagged with relevant metadata to appear on the page automatically, or fresh content added to the page to appear elsewhere, depending on how the taxonomy is deployed.

Category menus and tag lists
These allow users to choose a category for content they create before they post it. Users may select from a drop-down menu or, where the category list is much larger, enter free text and select from a series of suggestions. They are often used in knowledge repositories and may be mandated if the user wants to post, although this puts many users off. In some cases the knowledge manager adds tags after the content has been posted.

File plans
These are pre-coordinated lists which create places where documents can be saved. They are used to help documents to be found again and to enable retention and deletion criteria to be applied. As mentioned in Chapter 3, their chief weakness is that it is difficult to encourage people to use them.

Types of knowledge storage

Enquiries databases

A number of enquiry-based services, including libraries, record details of user interactions for future reference. In some cases they are an appendage to transactional databases needed to record service activity and justify staff numbers. They may be attached to a customer relationship management system such as Salesforce. In these cases the transaction logging takes place for a different purpose but, since it is happening anyway, useful information about the questions asked and work done to respond to them can be added. It is clear from speaking to professionals that such systems are used from time to time as reference sources. The chief challenge is to encourage staff to add to them in the course of a busy day. Doing so during the course of the transaction could be a physical barrier to serving staff and slow down fulfilment of the request. Adding the information later becomes an administrative burden for staff who have presumably been working hard at the front line. Some library management systems offer an enquiries module. Potentially these are likely to be better designed for easy use than an ad-hoc database and may interact with circulation data to add value to the information.

When implementing enquiries databases, you should balance the effort involved in maintaining them with the extent to which they are likely to be used. There is no point requiring staff to add information about how an enquiry was resolved if nobody then uses it in the future. Enquiries databases are probably most valuable not for the enquiries made every day (details of which should, when possible, be transferred to a wiki, public FAQ list or intranet) but those made often enough that the information source is forgotten. Try and choose a means of recording that requires the minimum effort for staff. If your service uses a few key information sources, populating a drop-down menu reduces the data entry burden and (if used consistently by staff) provides extra usage data when subscriptions are renewed. To be really useful, the database should have some kind of taxonomy, a very good free-text search or both. Categorisation is helpful if you receive a certain number of enquiries on the same topic and, again, drop-down menus can save users time. And enquiries databases are an excellent way of identifying changes in types and topics of request. The findings can then be used to refresh web content or develop new sources of online information for users.

Because enquiries databases are most useful for the middle category of enquiries, those that come between repetitive transactions and the long tail of unique requests, they are most suitable for certain types of service. Library or archive services with large research collections are a good example, as the range of enquiries will exceed the capacity of even expert researchers to retain in their heads. Collections with unique materials can also use them to help identify areas that may need cataloguing as a priority. And if you do need to record transactions for accountability purposes anyway, then adding some extra information about sources used need not be a significant extra burden.

Wikis

Wikis are a social media phenomenon (taking their name from the Hawaiian for 'fast') originally intended to remove editorial barriers to allow content to be made public and edited quickly. The most famous iteration, the online encyclopedia Wikipedia, allows registered users to edit pages and relies on combined efforts over time to ensure some measure of accuracy in the content, with a readily available audit trail in the background so that content additions are transparent. Wikipedia operates with increasing quantities of editorial control and its founders continue to encourage those with access to authoritative collections to add and edit pages. However, its premise is to offset speed against authority and to open up content creation to a wider range of users than traditional publishing processes allow.

Organizations use wikis in different ways. Some host their intranet on a wiki platform, others reserve it for particular areas of work. Certain teams or practice groups start their own wikis for internal guidance including not just formal manuals, but tricks, tips and frequently used resources or contacts. These can work very well as a means of enabling updates to take place quickly in a fast-changing environment. Crucially, they are not reliant on a named, senior person to sign off the content, but enable contribution from all members of the workforce. In the right culture, a wiki encourages participation from those who might be put off by a more formal process of documentation. And, as with other knowledge artefacts, you can encourage participation through offering prizes for numbers of contributions. This approach works particularly well to populate a wiki at its inception. However, encouraging users to continue to update the wiki is likely to be a challenge.

The fun aspect of wiki creation works well with certain workforces, such as technology employees, but is less likely to engage those in highly regulated professions such as law or accountancy. Wikis often grow up as grassroots initiatives among tech-savvy staff. We are particularly aware of early careers researchers in academia using those, and other KM initiatives, but there is little evidence at the time of writing that information professionals within their institutions initiate or support them.

As a knowledge manager, you can provide templates and structure for your colleagues to use, in a way that is far simpler than the creation of team sites, for example. And it should be simple for staff to add content too. It is worth thinking about the types of knowledge collections which benefit the most from widespread participation and setting up relevant wiki pages to be populated.

Knowledge maps and white pages

These are different means of representing the knowledge held within an organization through its people and departments. Roughly described, a knowledge map is likely to be a one-off exercise carried out by the knowledge manager and white pages are something that staff continually add to themselves. They should represent who knows what in an organization, and provide a resource for connecting people with a knowledge need to the relevant expertise.

Knowledge maps are the knowledge equivalent of the audit and similarly should have a firm purpose in mind. Organizational knowledge changes constantly so any record is likely to go out of date immediately after it has been created. However, a knowledge map can be immensely valuable in identifying shared areas of knowledge and gaps. On an everyday level, it can give you the confidence to put people in touch with each other when moderating forums or communities of practice. At a higher level, knowledge maps can help guide training and hiring strategy, or even spark a reorganization. Used in conjunction with benchmarking tools, and competitor intelligence, staff can use knowledge maps to identify your organization's unique selling points in the market or spot weaknesses. But for these outcomes to occur, senior staff must identify improving staff knowledge and competitiveness as a need to begin with.

White pages (sometimes called yellow pages) are essentially staff directories. Ideally their basis is some form of staff master data drawn from HR systems. In Microsoft houses, they are commonly powered by the service Active Directory, although most Active Directory implementations are of such poor quality that very little data can be drawn from them. Sadly this is often true of all master data held about staff. Even where it was accurately entered (onto an HR or IT system) at the point the employee joined the organization (not guaranteed if this task is given to low-paid staff), it goes out of date as the employee progresses. The responsibility of updating information such as job title, reporting lines and physical location can fall between old and new line managers, IT support staff, HR staff and employees themselves and very often no updates are made. This is worth addressing from a knowledge capture point of view, but also very important for information security purposes, as staff may continue to have access to systems and data they no longer need.

Assuming your staff data is sufficient to power a directory with information populated automatically from the staff record, your next stage when creating white pages is to encourage staff to enrich the information. The point of white pages is to record both the expertise staff practice in their job, and extra skills they may be happy to share with others in the workplace. A classic example is language skills. I have a document I need to read in a language I don't understand. By consulting my white pages I find that a colleague is a native speaker in that language. It is not their job to translate, but because they have shared this skill it can be used by the organization. The challenge with white pages, as with many knowledge artefacts, is to encourage people to populate it. This is one example where offering a short-term incentive, such as a prize for completing their entry, or for the team with the most entries completed, might be worthwhile. Gamification to encourage knowledge-sharing is less useful as an ongoing exercise but white pages are knowledge repositories which may not change that frequently.

As a knowledge manager it is your role to consider how much structure should go into each entry. If you provide a list of skills for employees to select from, you will have an excellently structured dataset of everyone who, for example, can code in a particular language, but might have missed the opportunity to record skills you have not thought of. Having lots of different fields to fill in can prompt employees to share lots of useful information, but the more time-consuming the exercise, the less people are likely to complete it. A good starting point is to consider how you would want to structure your own profile. You could also try trawling online discussion forums to see the types of skills need most frequently posted.

Knowledge bases

Knowledge bases are collections of useful content organized into categories. They may actually be designed as a database of terms, structured with a taxonomy and definitions supplied by appropriate areas of the business. Or they may be looser collections of pages managed to a greater or lesser extent by the knowledge team. They may bring together internal documents, external links, blog posts and other resources such as journal articles. They may host discussions on the topic or, where based around specific projects, include appropriate project documentation. Many of the points made about online communities of practice apply to knowledge bases – How much governance should be applied? How do you encourage staff to engage with them? – but where the focus of communities of practice should firmly be in the immediate interaction, knowledge bases benefit from more controls, structure and governance.

Our advice is to start from the information – unstructured or structured – that exists in the organization and consider how it could be better used to meet users' needs. One interviewee for this book implemented a structured team site collection which immediately found an enthusiastic audience and remains a popular resource. Its key was that it uncovered knowledge documents such as white papers, which were being underused, and brought them together with other resources in a searchable way. No previous online corporate resource had previously been available with the same search capability and staff were quick to recognise the value of the content now that they could find it. In this case a corporate taxonomy also helped to direct users to content they had not previously been aware of. However, as long as the right people can find the resources they need, you may be able to leave the structure and population of your knowledge base entirely to staff.

Some organizations benefit more than others from knowledge bases. A key mistake made in many knowledge programmes of the past decade has been to create knowledge bases as a means of having a tangible product. It is a natural instinct for information professionals in particular to want to have a tamed repository of knowledge. But for some organizations, the key moments of knowledge creation and exchange may not take place in these controlled locations. It is therefore essential to work with your user groups to find out whether they would actually use a pre-coordinated collection of content and how they want it structured, if at all. There is no point having a beautifully curated collection of discrete knowledge sites if the actual knowledge exchange takes place over Slack or in a discussion forum. However, if you do have a collection, it is worthwhile finding ways of pointing it out to anyone who might benefit, for example, by joining in a discussion and pointing them to the relevant knowledge site or database item.

Certain users are more natural candidates than others to use and populate knowledge bases. Any profession that has a set of established practices which are open to change and reinterpretation is likely to embrace a topical repository with some control. The next section, 'Know-how pages', describes one type common in the legal sector. Areas whose staff routinely solve problems, such as IT departments, are also likely to benefit. And enquiry teams, including call centres, are likely to operate with knowledge bases, although they may be referred to as FAQs. Our advice is to see whether the current resources work for staff and help with advice and improvements. Don't forget to talk to staff at all levels and give them time to discuss issues without managers being present. Call centres in particular are subject to tight rules and procedures, which may or may not work for the staff using them. They are unlikely to complain in front of the manager who devised them or is responsible for enforcing them. But it is essential that knowledge repositories meet users' actual needs, rather than those that it is thought they should have.

Gaining user engagement is a key issue in all knowledge projects. However, instead of building a knowledge repository and publicising it, you can connect staff to knowledge through personalisation. As mentioned in 'Knowledge organizing systems', individual staff members can be associated with particular information needs. For example, members of an e-mail group or attendees at a particular committee could be associated with tags taken from taxonomies. Content tagged with relevant terms will appear to them when it is added. As with the white pages example above, you need excellent staff master data to be able to ensure that content is still relevant to the job that the employee actually does, rather than that recorded in Active Directory. Pushing only relevant content to users is an excellent way of increasing their access to knowledge without overloading them, but it needs to work well to gain users' trust, or they will ignore the content and go elsewhere. Another personalisation option is to use data about previous usage of resources (based on audit trails and search patterns) and build a profile of users' interests and needs. However, you need to be mindful of the legal framework for using employee data in your geographical territory. In the

UK, the Information Commissioner advises that workers are entitled to a degree of privacy at work, and that employers should be clear about the purpose of any data gathering and make users aware when it takes place. We will cover more about using data in our afterword.

Know-how pages

Know-how pages are popular in law firms. There the term 'know-how' is used to describe a range of knowledge and information tasks, but refers to a database or collection of pages around specific topics. The content is likely to be written by a legal expert, whether a professional support lawyer or a fee earner, and to have a firm editorial process and high level of authority. Know-how pages are often characterised as providing expert analysis on topics, distilling both the law and the firm's approach to it, but may include standardised documents such as templates and precedents. As Russell (2016) suggests, a commercial law firm sells its services not on the basis of information, which is available to everyone, but on the way it interprets and acts on it. In a law firm, therefore, the role of the knowledge manager is likely to be that of commissioner, editor and technical support and to add metadata or taxonomic structure. In other organizations, the knowledge manager may themselves originate content.

Staff in law firms often use know-how pages to house their precedent or template documents, which aim to be legal documents designed for particular practice areas to use as a first draft (some also use specimen documents, which are excellent examples of this). In a large firm, know-how pages tend to be drafted by professional support lawyers, with a robust editorial sign-off. They are key authoritative sources considered to be part of the firm's intellectual property. All types of organization can use the approach of housing their most precious and authoritative documents on know-how pages, while providing value with extra content (such as external links) on the same topic. In a technology or engineering organization, these might be white papers or other research and development documents. If know-how pages are made available to everyone, they offer staff the opportunity to access repositories of useful information and ensure access to the most authoritative versions of documents. Ideally the documents themselves are housed in a controlled central location and linked to from the pages.

The authors of this book have also used know-how pages for restricted groups. As with walled communities of practice, these are not the ideal model for knowledge-sharing but a way to enable collaboration between senior people without the need to transfer hard copy files, or multiple versions of documents shared as e-mail attachments. Over time, as they realise the innocuousness of

Case study 5.2: Managng legal know-how

A commercial law firm had allowed a set of know-how pages to develop organically, within practice areas with little governance. As a result, there was a plethora of similar know-how pages, many with very little content, others with significant quantities of out-of-date content, including documents. Generally, staff in practice areas set up a page for their own group but often lost interest and failed to maintain it. Content was largely producer-led, rather than by considering what colleagues might like to know.

As part of an organization-wide initiative to encourage staff to think more corporately, a new KM solution was implemented with far stricter controls. The new know-how pages were planned around topic areas which did not necessarily reflect the lines of practice areas (although they did in many cases). There were concerns from senior staff in some practice areas that people within the firm would use their content without understanding the complexity of the law. The phrase 'a little knowledge is a dangerous thing' was commonly used. Legal experts felt others in the firm should consult them in person should any questions related to their practice area arise. They were legitimately concerned that staff who had not carried out continuing professional development in their practice were not qualified to advise clients, and also concerned about losing billable hours to another practice area. Knowledge staff had to make sure that staff understood the difference between enlarging their own knowledge to advise better in their own area, and when to pass clients over to another part of the firm.

The new areas of the know-how pages contained a core of authored and edited content produced by professional support lawyers, legal precedents and specimens, and other content related to the practice area and client-base. In addition to pages largely used by specific practice areas, there were other, cross-practice pages and some devoted to particular geographical regions. All pages were visible to all areas, although by mutual understanding people would not add content to the pages of specific practice areas other than their own. Although page creation was mandated by a request form sent to the knowledge team, it was rare for a new page to be refused. Some offices had larger collections of pages than others, suggesting cultural tendencies (or perhaps, given that the pages were all in English, a language preference).

The new set of know-how pages was a huge improvement on the previous collection. Authoritative content was approved, up to date and visible to everyone in the firm. Sites were mostly only set up if there was a unique need for them so there was far less duplication and far fewer unmaintained sites. Setting up the sites in and of themselves could not tackle the lack of trust between practice areas, but the knowledge team worked hard to ensure that the highest quality content was available to all staff, and would only be used appropriately.

most of the content, staff may be prepared to share the information with a wider group within the organization. Another approach, available on SharePoint team sites, is for an individual page to display web parts with different levels of security. Users can be secure in the knowledge that only a select few can see documents they consider to be secret while sharing less sensitive material.

Know-how pages offer a curated space for people to share highly valuable knowledge. They work well as collaboration spaces, offering a single space to share documentation and background information. They are a great opportunity for knowledge managers to bring in relevant content that users may not have thought about. For example, one of the authors of this book used SharePoint web parts to uncover their index of in-house journal articles. Provided the site owner used the correct index term when the site was set up, relevant article references appeared as soon as they were indexed. Of course the user did not always get the term correct, often capitalising or hyphenating in a different way from the author, but the knowledge that the articles would appear was an incentive for them to try.

Recommended approaches

An organization's knowledge repositories may contain its most valuable and highly curated knowledge content. As a knowledge manager, you can curate trusted repositories, which staff can add to without waiting for any formal publication mechanism. As a knowledge manager, you can enhance with a taxonomical structure, enabling relevant content to be found serendipitously without people needing to know it exists. However, we feel that knowledge repositories should operate alongside other less structured knowledge platforms, such as discussion forums and internal social media. If you have made staff reasonably aware that knowledge repositories exist, but they still prefer to ask colleagues questions, this suggests that such questioning is their preferred mechanism for knowledge-sharing. This is not to say that there is no place for authoritative, stable content organized by topic. But it should work hand in hand with online communities and, where appropriate, one-on-one transactions.

Further reading

Lippell, H. (2014) Building a corporate taxonomy. In Schopflin, K. (ed.), *A Handbook for Corporate Information Professionals*, Facet Publishing, 57–76.

Russell, H. (2016) A Law Firm Librarian's Guide to KM, *Legal Information Management*, **16**, 131–37.

Chapter 6

Capturing knowledge legacy: passing on staff knowledge

This chapter looks at techniques to capture organizational legacy knowledge. The approaches taken in the book so far all do this to some extent, but this chapter highlights the risks of unconsidered staff turnover and what you can do to prevent corporate knowledge disappearing. We look at two approaches to ensure that the most valuable staff knowledge and information does not disappear over time.

In his 2002 article, Wilson said 'whatever businesses claim about people being their most important resource, they are never reluctant to rid themselves of that resource (and the knowledge it possesses) when market conditions decline'. The modern workplace is characterised by a high staff turnover, frequent restructures and in some organizations an internal competition and blame culture. This all has the potential to lead to knowledge disappearing from organizations without anyone noticing. Moreover, in an environment where employees struggle to keep their jobs, and have to reinvent themselves with every restructuring, there is little motivation to share professional secrets.

Efficient HR managers design job roles to be interchangeable. This enables staff to transfer easily when vacancies become available and allows natural wastage without redundancy payments. But it does not encourage sharing. If I am not identified by the special knowledge I bring to this job, or have acquired during its course, what motivation do I have to create a legacy? Temporary and zero hour contracts exacerbate the problem of knowledge loss. Staff in those circumstances may be perpetually looking for another job, even where they feel a commitment to the organization they currently work for. It is rare for managers in many organizations to take a considered approach to the problem when staff leave. And where they do, they usually concentrate on positions in the upper echelons. Corporate hierarchies conceal the fact that essential corporate knowledge can be embodied in quite junior people. These people leave organizations without much attention.

Recognition of this problem is not new. Beazley, Boenisch and Harden's book *Continuity Management* predicted a demographic time bomb in the USA as the baby boomer generation retired, taking their expertise and knowledge with them (2002, 9). They identified what they called 'knowledge continuity' as essential for organizations to maintain their competitive advantage (51–3). They argued that articulating the knowledge of existing staff and finding ways to pass it on improves:

* staff identity and commitment
* new staff induction processes
* informed decision-making
* training and organizational learning
* staff turnover rates
* the strength of knowledge networks
* knowledge-sharing
* institutional memory
* creativity and innovation
* contingency planning and organizational sustainability
* customer experience and commitment.

Effectively, staff in organizations with good continuity management understand their jobs and organizational mission well, feel valued, know whom to talk to and can focus on doing their jobs well and coming up with new ideas. These organizations have lower staff turnover and can trust newer staff to take over when older staff leave.

The problem is not limited to staff departures. Left to themselves, organizations have short memories. Even where core values or a mission statement are articulated, focus moves from priority to priority and today's important project can be a distant memory in a few years. Perhaps it is even an embarrassment, a failure, which surviving participants are hoping everyone will forget. Yet if staff in organizations acknowledge these experiences they can learn and improve the way they approach problems in the future.

Capturing the experience, knowledge and wisdom of staff at all levels of the organization is an essential part of KM. Some of the methods covered in previous chapters are designed to do this. Anything that encourages knowledge to be articulated and shared will help the flow of knowledge, whether formally or informally. However, the approaches in this chapter concentrate specifically on two methods of capturing employee legacy. The first covers 'pause points' during projects and ongoing activities. There are techniques for asking staff to stop and consider what went wrong, what went well and what could be done differently in the future in relation to a project or activity. These are sometimes known as 'lessons learned' or 'after-action reviews' but can also be embodied in storytelling, 'brown-bag lunches' and sessions of 'show and tell'.

The second method of capturing employee legacy concerns what happens when staff move through and leave organizations. Can any of their expertise be captured, or will it vanish as soon as they no longer embody the role in question? Is it worth wading through the vast quantity of recorded information most employees create during their careers? And should we concentrate on executives when they leave, or put as much work into capturing the legacy of long-serving staff at junior levels?

Most of the approaches to KIM in previous chapters have been large-scale initiatives designed to encourage KIM among larger groups, or at least to be capable of widespread dissemination. The techniques in this chapter are more bespoke: encouraging smaller groups to share information face to face, or concentrating on the output of a single person or department. It is useful to think of KIM as a type of research in this context. Large-scale many-to-many projects are like quantitative research: their value comes from the number of people they involve. Many of the approaches in this chapter are like qualitative research, where the value comes from the depth, specificity and relevance of the content shared.

Storytelling and 'show and tell'

What we call 'storytelling' in this chapter covers a range of face-to-face activities involving staff sharing learning from recent work activities. When and how these take place, and how far it is mandated, varies from organization to organization. Here are some examples from the authors' own experiences.

Monthly brown-bag lunches

These were highly curated talks given by members of the knowledge team in collaboration with a subject expert. They were given three times, at each of the different sites where the organization was based. Each session consisted of a formal presentation followed by discussion. Attendance was not mandated but was encouraged for certain groups of staff. Staff with a particular interest in the topic were usually good attenders. One very specific topic, on a controversial project of concern to one team, sparked a heated discussion. While attendance was not huge at this event, it allowed people to air views that had been considered off-message, but which the project member (the subject expert in this case) could not now ignore. Such opportunities to share knowledge outside standard work procedures can be stimulating and highlight topics which might usually be overlooked.

Demo retros

Demo retros are regular events for those using agile methodology (as outlined in Agile Alliance, nd) to share the achievements of the previous sprint (a period of time during which particular work has to be completed; see below for more about agile methodology and sprints). In one company sprints were a two-week period in which staff were assigned achievable tasks related to broader aims. In its early years, this company allowed each team to share what it had achieved over the fortnight. As it grew, staff found this took too long, and restricted it only to teams who had something significant or new to share or who had completed a longer-term task. While sprints remained a positive group bonding exercise for the company, it is difficult to say how much staff learned from each other, especially once many of them were no longer permitted to share. End-of-sprint demo retros are perhaps most effective in a tightly knit technical environment with a clearly shared focus.

Storytelling events

The authors have experienced storytelling events as ad-hoc and optional activities, where a member of staff gives a narrative account of a recent activity and what they learned from it. Attendance was usually better where sessions took place in work time, rather than the employees' lunch hour. Not adhering to any specific programme or topical constraint, these were useful and provocative on an individual level. They covered such topics as case studies, project reviews and tales from the front line. Some organizations hold these more frequently than others; organizing them is a core part of the knowledge manager's job.

Weekly show and tell sessions

Weekly show and tell sessions were compulsory in one organization for everyone over a certain level, and encouraged for everyone else in the directorate. Those covering recent workstreams in different parts of the directorate were held in work time, but during the lunchtime period. They usually attracted a large audience, as staff were young and enthusiastic, but how far they actually conveyed value is difficult to say, given the diversity of topics addressed.

Question and answer forums

Storytelling doesn't have to take place face to face. Some technology such as Jive allows for dedicated time-specific discussion forums and knowledge-sharing sessions. They work best when they are curated or facilitated, so that discussions remain on topic.

Recommended approaches

Much is written in the information world about how to attract people to training sessions such as those discussed above through incentives such as treats, or via a culture of example (senior people will see me if I turn up). But we think the best results occur when the event is highly relevant to staff concerns. For this reason, a brown-bag lunch with eight highly engaged attendees could be far more valuable than a weekly learning or show-and-tell session attended by 75% of staff whose concentration is patchy and interest low. In the former case, a conversation is more likely to emerge and a genuine engagement with the topics ensues. Whichever approach your organization takes, always remember that staff are giving up time to attend, whether that is time that would otherwise be spent achieving the work tasks for which they are measured, or their own free time.

After-action reviews and lessons learned

After-action reviews are learning events where participants in a project or new operation are asked to reflect on recent activities. They are sometimes known as 'lessons learned'. They differ from the activities discussed above in that they usually concern those directly involved in a project, rather than take the form of a demonstration to the whole organization. In some cases members of project teams are asked to keep diaries from the start of the project, to note down and reflect on specific things they learned, or which happened unexpectedly. The review event allows them to go through them either in a one-to-one situation with a manager or with a group. In some cases, a template is provided for the participant to fill in, which enables a consistent approach and reporting. However, this may turn the review into a dry, box-ticking exercise, particularly if it happens at the end of the project when the employee is ready to move on. After-action reviews work best when those involved are reflective and non-judgmental and understand that consequences are better when there is organizational understanding rather than individual blame.

Projects are ripe areas for knowledge capture as they are resource-intensive and often an organization's second largest annual area of financial expenditure after payroll. In an ideal world, the first stage of any project initiation would be for staff to learn from previous, similar projects. As Trees (2017a) suggests, 'Project teams benefit from learning what other teams have tried, replicating their successful innovations and avoiding their mistakes.' In companies such as consultancies, new projects may have similar deliverables to previous client engagements. There is clear value in transferring knowledge from one project to another, but surprisingly this rarely occurs. Although traditional waterfall projects, such as those using Prince 2 methodology, generate large quantities of records, they are in many ways not designed to generate knowledge and learning for the following reasons:

* *They are rigidly timetabled*: team members are keen to get going without prior reflection.
* *They often go over time*: an effort of will is needed to make teams genuinely reflect at pause points.
* *They involve temporary teams*: participants often disperse at different times without ever reflecting as a team.
* *They involve closed teams*: project teams are separate from the rest of the organization so information and documentation are unlikely to reach anyone outside that team.
* *There are limits of responsibility*: by the time a project closes members may have moved on, and the surviving ones are not motivated to dwell on what went right, and especially not on what went wrong.

Because project teams are often a resented, expensive team separate from the core business, it is hard to transfer project learning to daily activities. Trees (2018) suggests that different groups within an organization need differing levels of detail of knowledge to be shared depending on their level of involvement, though when a project has gone catastrophically wrong a detailed analysis may be necessary, which should be shared widely. Case study 6.1 outlines a follow up from a partially failed project, which resulted in a high degree of engagement to ensure the same mistakes were not repeated. It is relatively rare for managers to address the causes

Case study 6.1: Learning from failure

An organization which produced a large quantity of written content introduced an IM project designed to improve accessibility of content and efficiency of indexing. When the project started, the principal aim was to enable full text content to be accessed alongside its indexing. A secondary aim was to improve the efficiency of the indexing process, which was resource-intensive and had a poor balance of intellectual challenge to repetitive drudgery for the indexers. The option of abandoning indexing and instead simply offering a free-text search was considered but not pursued because of the complexity of abstract concepts represented and the perceived importance of the content.

Instead, a model of automatic indexing with some quality assurance was borrowed from a similar organization, which had reported vastly reduced indexing time and an opportunity for staff to carry out higher value work. Software was purchased which could connect the full text to its indexing terms and enable automated indexing. Unfortunately, once testing began, the quality of the automated indexing was considered insufficiently accurate and this part of the software was not implemented. Also unfortunately, because staff in the content creation department chose not to participate in the project, the transfer of data between their publishing system and the indexing system produced data with insufficient structure and poor formatting. Existing staff had to learn the new system, which was less well adapted to manual indexing, and more staff were recruited to clean up the data before it could be indexed.

Managers recognised that aspects of the project had failed and vowed not to repeat the same mistakes again. Before any new project could be initiated to improve IM, an analyst was appointed (from internal staff) to examine why an expensive costly project had failed to achieve its aims. The analyst looked in depth at the project's original aims, examined project documentation and interviewed participants. His main conclusion was that the secondary aim of automating indexing distracted from the benefit of aligning indexing to content. Had that been the main focus, the project would not have been attempted without involving content creators. The chief mistake of the project managers had been to develop an IM system to index content, which relied on importing the content without involving the content creators.

A second programme was planned at a far higher level and with buy-in from staff with connections to the content creators. The new project managers planned a series of projects, which would ensure that content would be accessible to all who needed it. The new programme took a master data approach to the content and ensured that information retrieval concerns were considered from the point of content creation. The successful outcome of this second programme can be directly related to the lessons learned from the first. Ironically, it was the expensive and resource-intensive failure of the first project which forced an engaged level of involvement and influence, and the content creators to align their needs to those of the information managers.

of a failed project, as it involves acknowledging failures of staff or teams who may still be in the organization. It is far more usual for project teams to disperse quietly back into the organization, project managers to move on to new projects and, perhaps, senior staff to move to another organization. It is brave for managers in an organization to examine a project's failures and learn from them.

This is one reason why many organizations at the time of writing (2018) are adopting a more or less agile approach (the term is used here in a looser sense than agile methodology as applied in software development, as many organizations take its iterative approach without adopting all aspects of it). Instead of a project planned with phases lasting months ahead, manageable chunks of work are identified. Sprints of a week to a month allow short-term objectives to be tackled and daily standups (short meetings where attendees stand to discuss progress on a project) enable immediate blockages to be identified and tackled. Instead of requiring after-action reviews and lessons learned, agile projects constantly reflect and improve, bringing learning into the weekly or fortnightly sprint cycle. However, this does not preclude combining an agile approach with more thorough reflective pauses. Lessons learned sometimes need time and distance to be fully realised and to be at their best point for sharing with the rest of the organization.

As with all KM products, project outputs are only useful if they help to inform future action. It is not enough to record after-project learning. It needs to be incorporated into ongoing and future activity. As projects usually involve the introduction of new technology or ways of working, they are areas where innovation and knowledge drawn from outside flourish. They may be the first place in an organization where new ways of thinking appear and it's important to transfer that knowledge into the organization. Finding ways to pass it to operational staff during the course of the project engages them and prepares them for changes. One approach is to establish a library to which teams must contribute during their projects. A well organized repository from previous projects can help new project teams as they start out to look at similar projects and identify risks and mitigations before they happen, as well as refer to reference material gathered in the course of previous projects. Creating a library as part of the project is worthwhile as long as there is evidence that staff working on future projects will consult it.

Trees (2017a) outlines several other approaches of passing on the knowledge gained during projects. For example, at the British multinational defence, security, and aerospace company BAE Systems, learning is collated at the end of the project schedule and incorporated into training courses, which participants in new projects are expected to attend. Another approach is to ensure that project learning is a standing item on strategic board agendas. This ensures that managers who shape future initiatives are exposed to the outcomes of past projects and forced to incorporate them into their risk assessments. The project management community can also reach out to operational staff and share progress at physical or online events. This type of engagement is useful both to help staff understand the work of the project and how it will affect them, and to ensure that the project's work remains relevant to the concerns of the organization.

Engineering companies are known to be particularly active in project reviews, perhaps because of the costs and potential risks of building and bespoke manufacturing projects, and the length of time they take. The end of a project might be too late for them to hold an after-action review. Trees (2018) shares car manufacturer Volvo's lessons learned methodology, applied at every 'stage gate' of every project, in a workshop-type setting. Participants:

* identify all project pain points and compile a list
* identify the root cause of each project issue
* evaluate whether each issue has potential implications for other project teams
* establish a corrective plan within the current project team
* identify possible improvements and log the lessons, root causes, improvements and potential recipients for this advice
* take each actionable improvement for committee review, which they then disseminate with other projects and ongoing operations
* take the project learning into their own areas, apply it and report back.

Having an honest culture about mistakes is an essential part of successful reviews. Too often the problems of implementing new projects are pushed to the side. Problems are recorded in issues logs but not often tackled if this would involve addressing systemic problems within the organization. If the project team cannot themselves solve issues of adoption or use, they may well ignore them – after all, the project is likely to close before the full outcome is apparent. The mistake project managers in many organizations make is to assume that resistance to project change among operational staff is simply evidence of personal conservatism and can therefore be ignored. An honest review at regular stages of a project stage gate should identify these problems and assess what can be done to mitigate them.

It can be a challenge for an operational knowledge and information manager to gain access to large-scale, prestigious projects, particularly in hierarchical and secretive organizational cultures. But by implementing techniques such as those outlined above, they can be the bridge between the project and the rest of the organization and prevent some very expensive mistakes from taking place. Moreover, project teams often contain the most adventurous people in the organization. If you can make contact, they may be more than happy to accept your advice and try out new approaches.

Knowledge capture from departing staff

It is a sad fact that departing employees are rarely consulted for their knowledge and expertise, through interview or audit. Sometimes this is hard to avoid. Where a knowledgeable member of staff moves to a competitor, they are usually asked to leave the same day, locked out of company systems and sent on gardening leave. Where staff leave after long-term sick leave there is rarely a chance to consider what they brought to their role. And where staff leave after compulsory redundancy or termination of a contract, they have very little motivation to share when, after all, it has been identified that their skills and knowledge were no longer of enough importance to the organization to maintain their employment. How much of a concern this is will depend very much on your organizational culture. If you already have a good sharing culture, the bulk of knowledge will have already been shared using any of the many techniques outlined in this book so far. Unfortunately, organizations with the most restrictive cultures are also those least likely to have a positive exit procedure.

At very senior level this can be more of a consideration (although as Friel and Duboff, 2009, point out, replacement executives may be resistant to learning from retiring staff). One of the interviewees for this book worked for a startup whose co-founder moved on after the company had reached its ninth birthday. This is a common pattern for entrepreneurs who get most pleasure out of the early years of building a company and in this case was clearly a long-thought-out decision. And yet, only after the co-founder had left did others in the company realise how much accumulated wisdom that person had held, which had not been recorded anywhere. This has alerted them to the need for an exit process for the next person who leaves. This is a small company with a high staff retention rate. Larger companies have more reason to be prepared to capture senior staff legacy.

Possible techniques you might use are handover and exit interviews, knowledge audits, recording oral history and archiving, all discussed below.

Handover and exit interviews

Where possible, a handover interview is always desirable, but it is impossible if the new employee has to serve a long contract notice with their previous employer. It is not uncommon for the contract of CEO-level staff to insist that, in return for compensation, they remain available for discussion for a number of months after leaving. Many may alternatively or additionally serve in a board capacity once their executive duties have finished. If a handover interview is impossible, or not desired by new incumbents, then some form of debriefing is desirable. Ideally this is incorporated into HR procedure and made clear at the point the employee is first hired. The role of the knowledge manager is to identify who carries out the exit interview, what is asked and what happens to the information. It could become a key part of the induction process for new staff.

Knowledge audits

The ultimate aim of a proactive knowledge audit is to understand where tacit knowledge exists in an organization and how it flows, rather than its content or what form it takes. A knowledge audit needs a lighter touch than an information audit, although your approach will be determined by the level of detail you need to obtain. You can capture this type of knowledge through one-to-one interviews, discussions or even electronic questionnaires.

Holding regular employee knowledge audits helps identify where gaps will appear if certain staff leave and can shape the company's recruitment strategy. This type of audit is worth undertaking if there has been a clearly articulated need at a high level but not if nobody is going to act on the results. An alternative approach, outlined by the organizational design firm NOBL (nd), is to identify the skills and knowledge without which the organization could not thrive at what it does, by surveying staff with the longest tenure. Benchmarking can also help you identify the knowledge that you need. Beazley, Boenisch and Harden suggest that building a knowledge continuity profile, a type of knowledge map, helps you identify who in your organization shares their knowledge with other people and where it comes to a stop (2002, 124–42). They also suggest that knowledge profiles should be identified for every job to identify what would be lost if the existing incumbent were to resign.

Various investigative approaches can help. The one you choose will depend on what is considered to be the biggest risk of knowledge loss in your organization. Ask these questions to find out what it is:

* What knowledge exists in the organization?
* What knowledge can we not do without?
* What knowledge do *all* staff need?
* What type of expertise do our most successful competitors employ?
* Who shares knowledge the most and what are their areas of expertise?
* What is the career profile of the key knowledge-holder in the organization?

Keep an open mind as you carry out these investigations. All employees make assumptions about who the most valuable staff are. You need to be ready to challenge those assumptions, rather than simply reproduce them.

As with all audits, it is essential that the lessons learned from them are put into action. Here are some examples:

* *Hiring*: Most organizations take staff departures as a checkpoint, often requiring that a business case is made to replace someone who has resigned. A better approach is to use audit findings to identify what knowledge you are likely to need in the future and plan your recruitment around it.
* *Onboarding*: At the point that they are recruited, staff should understand the different types of knowledge they need to do their jobs. Obviously staff bring the skills for which they were hired, but identifying the contextual knowledge they need and where they might find it (via people or written resources) will help them learn quickly and give them a positive initial experience.
* *Training*: Knowledge audits show up skills gaps which can be addressed by formal training, whether through classroom sessions, professional development, reading groups or simply peer-to-peer sharing.
* *Knowledge-sharing improvements*: If you have identified that staff in some areas of the organization share their knowledge only on a limited peer-to-peer basis, then you need to consider the tools and platforms that would enable them to spread their knowledge more widely. This may require significant culture change and will certainly need buy-in from senior staff, but having the tools ready is part of the process.
* *Offboarding (the separation process when employees leave a company)*: For the reasons outlined above, staff are rarely motivated to share before they leave and as most restructures are traumatic for them, knowledge capture is rarely a priority. Offering staff incentives for knowledge-sharing as part of

their leaving package may mitigate this – it is worth building this into strategies for departing staff.

As a knowledge manager you are likely to be unable to bring about these actions on your own. Decisions about knowledge audits need to be made at a strategic level as part of the recognition that legacy planning is an essential part of workforce management. But you can be ready to advise and suggest techniques such as those described above once the risks are recognised of letting staff depart without capturing their knowledge and expertise.

Oral history projects

Some organizations may have some form of recording the memories of veteran members of staff. Formal oral history projects are rare unless a corporate archivist is present, or an academic project has separately been funded to carry one out.

In either case, you and the subject need to know what is going to happen to any oral history recording. NOBL describes how NASA's recordings of veteran employees are played to new employees as part of their onboarding process, a powerful means of asserting company culture and drawing the new staff member into a sense of shared history (NOBL, nd). Many formal oral history projects, particularly those carried out in academia, are covered by confidentiality agreements where there is unlikely to be any transfer to current staff. The purpose is to create a record for the future and enable students to learn how organizations were run at a particular time in history. Interviews under these circumstances are freely given and uncensored, whereas if staff know transcripts will be shared they may sanitise their accounts. Particularly if they are retiring, staff may feel they have very little to lose by discussing things frankly and feel flattered by the interest taken in their achievements within the company.

Another approach is to produce two versions of an interview. This is most likely to happen if the interviews are taking place as part of an anniversary or souvenir history of an organization. The original unexpurgated interviews are kept securely and not shared without permission of the living data subject, but some knowledge is transferred by a professional writer or archivist into a published document.

Claudette John wrote five articles on oral history as part of a corporate archive programme with many practical tips for the Society of American Archivists in the late 1980s. These have been reprinted and are well worth consulting if you are considering an oral history approach in your organization. Claudette John's article for the Society of American Archivists (John, 1987) offers many practical tips which are useful to this day.

Archiving

Although expressed information is considered far less vulnerable than tacit knowledge when a staff member leaves, most organizations have few procedures to ensure business decisions and recorded knowledge of departing staff are managed in any useful way. In the days of paper records and document registries a reasonable quantity of recorded knowledge was captured, managed in the short to medium term, and sent to archive when appropriate. Today, even organizations with a formal archiving and records management function have very little control over the information created by staff and possibly no repository that allows electronic records to be retrieved in any long-term meaningful way.

As Chapter 3 suggested, e-mails can be a particular problem, as it is impossible to know how many valuable business records are retained in among the ephemera in an email repository. In some organizations staff are expected to save anything they need into a managed repository and there is an automatic deletion rule for e-mails. However, in some of these organizations no one feels empowered actually to delete e-mails as they feel it is too risky to destroy them; this can result in organizations having a vast archive of unstructured e-mails. Another method for dealing with e-mails is to adopt the 'Capstone approach', devised by the US National Archives and Records Administration (National

Case study 6.2: The Capstone approach

Organization B is a large corporate body with a long history and records management and archives functions. Since the emergence of e-mail, staff were concerned that many business decisions were not being captured comprehensively. During the period of hard copy registries, printed e-mails were captured where possible. Once an EDRM system was put in place, staff were advised to save their e-mails there, but this was not in any way mandated.

A departing senior member of staff with long service approached the archives team and offered their e-mail inbox as well as a large body of hard copy material to be assessed. They judged that their legacy was important and wanted to pass it on. This gave archives staff the idea to work with the information governance team, who were more prestigious in the organization, to create a policy for departing staff. The latter were concerned that records needed to be available for transparency purposes, but only kept for as long as necessary. Together, the archives and information governance staff wrote a paper suggesting that everyone who earned over a certain amount in the organization would have their mailbox audited when they left, and would be told about this policy when they joined. It was agreed that there were 'business continuity and archival reasons' for doing this. Although the suggestion was never officially adopted at board level, as members of the information governance team had co-authored the paper there was a strong impetus for this proposal to be put into practice.

When originally approached, the records management department concentrated on capturing the files, and a large body of .pst files were saved onto a PC desktop. Over time they developed the following process:

- A templated request for access to the mailbox is sent to information governance staff (with the tacit blanket approval of information security).
- An e-mail is sent to the departing staff member six weeks ahead of their departure date to give them an opportunity to delete personal material.
- An additional form is sent to the IT department in order for the transfer to take place.
- An identified IT staff member is given temporary access to enable transfer from the mailbox into a shared drive.
- E-mails over 90 days old have first to be retrieved from the archive vault and brought back into the mailbox before transfer.
- A member of records management staff then transfers all business e-mails into the EDRM system, deleting personal and generic all-staff e-mails as they go.

Some measure of sorting takes place. For example, when a long-serving staff member leaves, distinctions are made between the e-mails they have sent and received in different roles. Attachments are removed and saved separately unless a copy is already present. Once in the EDRM system e-mails can be searched by archives and records management staff to answer freedom of information, subject access, legal discovery and other requests. Initially access is only given to these staff, but can later be made available to staff taking over the departing employee's duties, and/or to their assistants.

Although it is identified as a business records process rather than an archival one – and the EDRM system is very much a holding location, as the organization does not yet have a digital archival repository – records are issued with an archival series description compliant with the ISAD(G) standard of the General International Standard Archival Description. Since the initial process was put into place, staff have captured the content of a large number of executive staff members' inboxes. The e-mails are now available where necessary in the short term and can be incorporated into future digital archiving processes. Only departing senior staff were captured initially, but lower-level staff in other strategic areas have since given the archives team access. Those in the records team have found a greater number of senior staff taking an interest because of concerns about data protection.

The process of capturing a vulnerable component of business information was made easier because it had the support and backing of staff working in an influential policy area within the organization. Although the technical process is far from ideal, access is managed in the medium term and the content has been captured to enable long-term storage and preservation.

Archives, 2013), which works on the assumption that capturing e-mails from a few key individuals will record most of the important interactions between executives in organizations – and captures items of importance from those lower down the chain. Case study 6.2 describes an example of this in action.

When staff leave an organization, the first challenge for information managers is to gain access to documents, e-mails and other material they have been working on. Some records staff may be given this automatically, others may need sign-off at a sufficiently high level. Managers in some organizations feel that – although they are the property of the organization – sharing documents created by an ex-employee breaches trust, particularly as personal documents are likely to be mixed up with business records. The low status of archive staff compared with senior executive staff may also be a barrier.

Once access to the documents of a recently departed staff member has been achieved, it can be a challenge to identify which ones are worth keeping and find a place to access them from. In case study 6.2 an EDRM system is used; Google Vault is another medium-term option. In any case, you will want to save as much metadata (such as time of creation and original save location) as is available from the original documents (for this reason, SharePoint is not a good option for this type of storage). Unless you choose to delete everything after a number of years, you may also want to find a digital preservation solution for the long-term archiving of records. Whatever is kept, a decision needs to be made about who has access and for what reason.

Recommended approaches

We have only scratched the surface of the potential for capturing and providing access to employee legacy. There is a host of records management practices we have not explored for written records. We hope we have demonstrated in this chapter that there is a place for strategic legacy capture, in addition to the more or less formal approaches to sharing and corralling useful knowledge we discussed in chapters 4 and 5. Ideally this should be built in to processes for recruitment, training, project management and workforce management. But the challenge for the knowledge manager in the current climate is to encourage managers to appreciate what they will lose if they ignore it.

Further reading

Beazley, H., Boenisch, J. and Harden, D. (2002) *Continuity Management: preserving corporate knowledge and productivity when employees leave*, John Wiley.

Friel, T. J. and Duboff, J. (2009) The Last Act of a Great CEO, *Harvard Business Review*, January, https://hbr.org/2009/01/the-last-act-of-a-great-ceo [accessed 8 May 2018].

John, C. (1987–9) Oral History as Part of a Corporate Archives Program, *Business Archives Section Newsletter*, www2.archivists.org/sites/all/files/John_OralHisCorpProg_0.pdf [accessed 8 May 2018].

NOBL (nd) How to Retain Knowledge When an Employee Leaves, *The Future of Work is Here*, http://futureofwork.nobl.io/future-of-work/tpljczhne9sll4gaeukkweoskxyz3u [accessed 8 May 2018].

Trees, L. (2017a) Project teams and KM, Part 1, Organizations win when project teams learn from collective experience, *KM World*, 17 September, www.kmworld.com/Articles/Editorial/Features/Project-teams-and-KM-%E2%80%93-Part-1—Organizations-win-when-project-teams-learn-from-collective-experience-120391.aspx [accessed 4 June 2018].

Trees, L. (2018) Project Teams and KM: part 3, the benefits of identifying and sharing lessons learned across projects, *KM World*, 22 January, www.kmworld.com/Articles/Editorial/Features/Project-teams-and-KM-Part-3—The-benefits-of-identifying-and-sharing-lessons-learned-across-projects-122653.aspx [accessed 4 June 2018].

Afterword: the future of knowledge and information management

The robots are coming. . . . Well, in truth they are already here and doing quite nicely. At the time of writing, one of the authors of this book was well advanced in implementing an artificial intelligence (AI) program to deliver self-service and self-help functionality to an employee portal. The project involved users engaging not with a traditional search box, or through a navigation aid, nor even connecting directly with an HR team agent, instead interrogating a chatbot. The chatbot will have direct access to the HR portal and its knowledge base, with policies and instructions, but it will also be able to query the HR engine which governs processes such as annual leave. If required, it can also interrogate the learning and development platform to point users to training manuals or courses in order to help them to complete a task. If a user asks 'How do I find out how much leave I have?', the chatbot will point them to their annual leave page and share a link showing how to submit annual leave requests. If they ask questions such as 'Can I take annual leave tomorrow?', the chatbot can bring up the relevant policy.

This fairly simple machine learning approach is just the start of what AI may be able to do to connect people to the knowledge they need. None of it is possible without the intervention of a knowledge manager to implement the business rules metadata which connect the question to the information. If you tell the bot to look for certain tags, or even natural language formulations, it can create connections both at the point of searching and by adding content to news feeds. However, beware of the salesperson who tells you their AI is capable of building the business rules and indexes for itself. The authors are yet to see a solution even close to having this capability. Like any human knowledge worker the chatbot or AI still needs to be taught. But once it learns, it can process a huge quantity of data at great speed. The next stage would be for the bot not simply to point to a relevant policy, but to actually answer the question and anticipate that the next thing the user wants to do is book some annual leave. Users no longer need a how-to guide, as the machine will carry out transactions for them, referencing what it knows about them from their profile (do they get long-service leave? Are they based in a territory with different rules, or from a legacy organization with special terms and conditions?).

Does this spell the end of HR policy guidance? No. The machine can only follow the rules it is given. At this stage machine learning is not yet sophisticated enough to second guess and understand what the user does not know it should know. However technology in this space is moving fast. We have deliberately chosen annual leave as the example here as HR-related questions apply to all employees (even those who don't qualify for annual leave). The development required for most AI projects is such that it is only worth undertaking for regularly repeated transactions. The more bespoke a knowledge-seeking process, the less likely it is going to be automated. Self-service and self-help systems lend themselves to call centres and customer support environments relatively simply, but only where the staff are themselves low-paid and not expected to deviate from scripts (beware, however, of the hidden value that customer service operatives add where they do bring nuance to their transactions). Human agents can benefit from working with chatbots where they are giving advice on querying complex policies or procedures. Machine learning can be used to support agents and guide them through different situations at speed.

Machine learning is in some ways KM writ large. Like Amy Liptrot's family sheep cited in Chapter 2, AI algorithms learn the best places to go over time and from experience. A chatbot can potentially learn from potentially hundreds of similar conversations to access knowledge which a human would struggle to remember. AI is currently expensive to implement but, once trained, AI programs can handle a huge number of queries at speed and never sleep. After a short period of time AI could become cheaper than a human counterpart carrying out work of relatively low value.

However, AI only solves big picture problems. At this stage it is best used where the aim is to uncover relevant content quickly, particularly where large bodies of new content are likely to be added. It cannot automate very bespoke queries and is not – yet – brilliant at understanding nuance and context, so is only as good as the questions you have asked it. It can tell you all the examples of where a certain type of project was implemented in the past, but only you can work out whether the project was a success and what can be learned from it. We should look to the large quantity of money spent on enterprise searches in the first decades of the 21st century. Powerful (and expensive) search tools did not solve the problem of our not being able to find the information we need from the huge quantity created.

We think there are three main applications of AI to the KIM world. The first is outlined above: where AI can connect people to the answers to their questions. It works like a very sophisticated search engine, rather than ranking results based on vocabulary matching, it applies a range of complex rules to large bodies of data.

The second relates to the worst problems of IM: the proliferation of information in multiple repositories with no context or metadata. As information managers, we try to encourage staff to classify their content at the point they create it, so we can put it in places where it could be found and, eventually, deleted. We frequently fail to do this. Instead we have managed repositories containing a fraction of organizational information and vast swathes of unstructured data with no rules applied at all. Given the right training, a powerful machine learning application could identify content in multiple locations, classify it and set up rules for deletion. It may not be perfect but would certainly be an improvement on the present. The ability of AI to interrogate unstructured data could also uncover hidden content as there may be more data points in unstructured data than you think. AI could help to find more of these by using one or more algorithmic criteria and enable you to obtain more value.

The third application is to drive personalised interfaces, giving users access to information of interest. In theory this happens already. Information and advertising is pushed to you constantly based on previous searching behaviour and other data mined about you. However, data used for advertising purposes is very different from that used in an HR context. Whatever your HR systems know about you (where you work, your role, the meetings you attend, your level of seniority) could be used to make sure you see the information you need, though this depends on such information being entered accurately to begin with and updated as you move through the organization. Over time, your profile could also be built up through your interactions with company systems and social networks. Beware though that this will only connect relevant knowledge to staff who choose to interact. Many employees feel that the exchange of money for their labour does not include their employer gathering any more data about them than necessary.

AI is not the only technological development likely to change how we manage and share information. Twenty years ago e-mail and internet use were heavily restricted in most workplaces. The authors of this book grew up at a time when our hunger for knowledge could only be satisfied by the published materials, or knowledgeable people, we were able to access. We are not able to predict the applications that will shape how we communicate and search in the future. We prefer not to make generalisations about different age groups, because age is usually less of a factor in how people behave than context, but people entering the workplace at the time of writing (2018) have been accustomed to using technology to access knowledge and information instantly. This is not a simple equation. As mentioned before, new entrants into the workplace do not have the power to transform it and may simply assume that workplace technology, communication and knowledge-seeking is different from the technology they use in their personal lives. But it is an opportunity for those who shape organizational KIM to challenge staff's perceptions and world views. Organizational leaders and managers in organizations pay lip service to diversity but they need to listen to different voices and welcome those with different life experiences into their businesses. What can we learn from how different people connect to knowledge and information?

In this afterword, we have not felt the need to question the need for KIM. All the factors - information needs, staff behaviour, technological shortcomings - things that existed and were true at the point that the KM and IM disciplines emerged are still here and remain true. We need the best access to the best tacit and expressed knowledge we can in order to carry out our work. It may not be done under the label 'knowledge management' or 'information management', but enabling people to access the people and content they need remains an essential role. How we will do it in the future remains to be seen.

References

Agile Alliance (nd) *Agile 101*, www.agilealliance.org/agile101/ [accessed 19 May 2018].

Bateson, G. (1972) *Steps to an Ecology of Mind: collected essays in anthropology, psychiatry, evolution, and epistemology*, University of Chicago Press.

Beazley, H., Boenisch, J. and Harden, D. (2002) *Continuity Management: preserving corporate knowledge and productivity when employees leave*, John Wiley.

Catone, J. (2007) BIF-3: Euan Semple – Bringing Social Networking to the BBC, *Readwrite*, 11 October, https://readwrite.com/2007/10/11/bif-3_euan_semple_-_social_networking/ [accessed 24 February 2018].

Cervo, D. and Allen, M. (2011) *Master Data Management in Practice: achieving true customer MDM*, Wiley.

Daland, H. (2016) Managing knowledge in academic libraries, Are we? Should we? *LIBER Quarterly*, **26** (1), 28–41, http://doi.org/10.18352/lq.10154.

Davenport, T. and Prusak, L (1998) *Working Knowledge*, Harvard Business School Press.

Friel, T. J. and Duboff, J. (2009) The Last Act of a Great CEO, *Harvard Business Review*, January, https://hbr.org/2009/01/the-last-act-of-a-great-ceo [accessed 8 May 2018].

Handy, C. (1976) *Understanding Organizations*, Penguin.

Hawley Committee (The) (1995) *Information as an Asset: a consultative report: the board agenda*, KPMG IMPACT Programme.

IFLA (2012) Potential of knowledge management in public libraries, *IFLA World Library and Information Congress: 78th IFLA General Conference and Assembly*, 14 August, Helsinki, Finland, www.ifla.org/past-wlic/2012/session-141.htm [Accessed 6 January 2018].

Information Commissioner's Office (2017) *GDPR and Accountability*, speech given to

Institute of Chartered Accountants in England and Wales, 17 January, https://ico.org.uk/about-the-ico/news-and-events/news-and-blogs/2017/01/gdpr-and-accountability/ [accessed 3 February 18].

John, C. (1987–9) Oral History as Part of a Corporate Archives Program, *Business Archives Section Newsletter*, www2.archivists.org/sites/all/files/John_OralHisCorpProg_0.pdf [accessed 8 May 2018].

Lindsay, D. (2014) Communities of Practice for the Post Recession Environment, NetIKX event, 16 September, https://netikx.wordpress.com/2014/09/22/communities-of-practice-for-the-post-recession-environment-tuesday-16th-september-2014/ [accessed 25 March 2018].

Lippell, H. (2014) Building a corporate taxonomy. In Schopflin, K. (ed.), *A Handbook for Corporate Information Professionals*, Facet Publishing, 57–76.

Liptrot, A. (2016) *The Outrun*, Canongate.

Loughborough University (2013) *Email – yet more stress at the office?*, 4 June, www.lboro.ac.uk/media-centre/press-releases/2013/june/email—yet-more-stress-at-the-office.html [accessed 3 February 2018].

Marulanda-Carter, L. (2013) *Email Stress and Its Management in Public Sector Organizations*, PhD thesis, Loughborough University, https://dspace.lboro.ac.uk/2134/14196.

National Archives (2013) Guidance on a New Approach to Managing Email Records, *Bulletin 2013–02*, 29 August, www.archives.gov/records-mgmt/bulletins/2013/2013-02.html [accessed 8 May 2018].

NOBL (nd) How to Retain Knowledge When an Employee Leaves, *The Future of Work is Here*, http://futureofwork.nobl.io/future-of-work/tpljczhne9sll4gaeukkweoskxyz3u [accessed 8 May 2018].

O'Reilly, T. and Battelle, J. (2005) What Is Web 2.0: design patterns and business models for the next generation of software, *O'Reilly*, 30 September, www.oreilly.com/pub/a/web2/archive/what-is-web-20.html [accessed 10 February 2018].

Orna, E. (1999) *Practical Information Policies*, Gower.

Orna, E. (2004) *Information Strategy in Practice*, Gower.

Russell, H. (2016) A Law Firm Librarian's Guide to KM, *Legal Information Management*, **16**, 131–7.

Schopflin, K. (2015) Success in Knowledge Management: against the revolutionary approach. In *Proceedings of the SLA Annual Conference 2015*, Special Libraries Association.

Schopflin, K. (2017) Networking for Best Effect – whether or not it comes naturally,

Jinfo, 8 June, https://web.jinfo.com/go/sub/article/73906 [accessed 4 June 2018].

Seddon, J. (2014) *The Whitehall Effect: how Whitehall became the enemy of great public services – and what we can do about it*, Triarchy Press.

Seely Brown, J. and Duguid, P. (2000) *The Social Life of Information*, Harvard Business School Press.

Teng, S. and Hawamdeh, S. (2002) Knowledge Management in Public Libraries, *Aslib Proceedings*, **54** (3), 188-197 https://doi.org/10.1108/00012530210441737.

Townley, C. T. (2001) Knowledge Management and Academic Libraries, *College & Research Libraries*, **62** (1), 44–55.

Trees, L. (2017a) Project teams and KM, Part 1, Organizations win when project teams learn from collective experience, *KM World*, 17 September, www.kmworld.com/Articles/Editorial/Features/Project-teams-and-KM-%E2%80%93-Part-1—Organizations-win-when-project-teams-learn-from-collective-experience-120391.aspx [accessed 4 June 2018].

Trees, L. (2017b) Project teams and KM – Part 2, Using communities and networks to share knowledge across products, *KM World*, 20 October, www.kmworld.com/Articles/Editorial/Features/Project-teams-and-KM-%E2%80%93-Part-2—Using-communities-and-networks-to-share-knowledge-across-products-121270.aspx [accessed 4 June 2018].

Trees, L. (2018) Project Teams and KM: part 3, the benefits of identifying and sharing lessons learned across projects, *KM World*, 22 January, www.kmworld.com/Articles/Editorial/Features/Project-teams-and-KM-Part-3—The-benefits-of-identifying-and-sharing-lessons-learned-across-projects-122653.aspx [accessed 4 June 2018].

Vascarello, J. (2009) Why Email No Longer Rules… And What That Means for the Way We Communicate, *Wall Street Journal*, 12 October.

Webb, J. (2008) *Strategic Information Management: a practitioner's guide*, Chandos.

Weinberger, D. (2005) The BBC's low-tech KM, *KM World*, 1 September, www.kmworld.com/Articles/Column/David-Weinberger/The-BBCs-low-tech-KM-14276.aspx [accessed 24 February 2018].

Wenger, E. (1998) *Communities of Practice: learning, meaning, and identity*, Cambridge University Press.

Wiig, K. M. (1997) Knowledge Management: an introduction and perspective, *Journal of Knowledge Management*, **1** (1), 6–14, https://doi.org/10.1108/13673279710800682.

Wilson, T. D. (2002) The Nonsense of Knowledge Management, *Information Research*, **8** (1), 144–54.

Wilson, T. D. (2005) The Nonsense of Knowledge Management Revisited. In

Macevičūtė, E. and Wilson, T. (eds), *Introducing Information Management: an information research reader*, Facet Publishing, 151–64.

Index

after-action reviews, legacy knowledge
    95–100
AI (artificial intelligence) 108–111
approaches
    governance 32–3, 43–9, 51–2
    knowledge repositories 90
    knowledge-sharing 72–3
    legacy knowledge 95–106
    online communities 72–3
    taxonomies 78–81
approaches to KIM 18–24
    problem solving 19–22
    synthesised approach 7
archiving, legacy knowledge 104–6
areas of emphasis, KIM 7
artificial intelligence (AI) 108–111
asset registers, information asset registers,
    governance 50–1
audits
    information audits, governance 45–7
    knowledge audits, legacy knowledge 101–3

Capstone approach, legacy knowledge, case
    study 104–5
case studies
    Capstone approach 104–5
    champions model/network 67–8
    core organizational data 31
    e-mail 36
    how not to introduce KIM 22
    indexing 97
    know-how pages 89
    knowledge repositories 31, 36
    knowledge-sharing 79–80
    learning from failure 97

legacy knowledge 97
making KIM noticed 18
online communities 62–3
SharePoint 79–80
taxonomies 79–80
users' language 79–80
challenges, KIM 8, 17–19
champions model/network
    case study 67–8
    knowledge-sharing 66–8
chat, knowledge repositories 37
chatbots 108–9
classification, taxonomies 78–81
communication
    knowledge repositories 30–3
    knowledge-sharing 56–68
    workplace 56–68
communities of interest, knowledge-sharing
    65
communities of practice 53–4, 61–5
    see also knowledge-sharing
    advantages 64–5
    benefits 61
    building the community 69–70
    facilitating the community 70–1
    knowledge-sharing 68–72
    online communities 61–4
    recording output 71–2
    Wenger, E. 61–4
    Wilson, T. D. 54
communities of purpose, knowledge-sharing
    66
consulting users, introducing KIM in
    organizations 20
controls, governance 40

core organizational data, knowledge
     repositories, case study 31
corporate policies, governance 42–3

data management, knowledge repositories
     30–3
data protection policies, governance 42–3
data repositories *see* knowledge repositories
databases, enquiries databases 82–3
definitions
     IM 2–3
     KIM 1–3
Denham, Elizabeth 42–3
discussion forums
     knowledge-sharing 57–60
     talk.gateway 58
     tools 59–60
diversity
     introducing KIM in organizations 19
     need for KIM 16

e-mail
     case study 36
     e-mail alternatives 37–9
     knowledge repositories 35–7
enquiries databases, knowledge storage 82–3
existing communities, introducing KIM in
     organizations 19
exit interviews, legacy knowledge 101
experience, introducing KIM in organizations
     23
expert advisers, organizational culture 14

file plans, governance 47–9
freedom of information legislation 6
future of KIM 108–111

General Data Protection Regulation (GDPR)
     6
     governance 6, 42–3
governance 25–52
     approaches to governance 32–3, 43–9, 51–2
     controls 40
     corporate policies 42–3
     data protection policies 42–3
     Denham, Elizabeth 42–3
     file plans 47–9
     General Data Protection Regulation
          (GDPR) 6, 42–3
     Hawley Report 5, 26
     IM advice 41
     information asset registers 50–1
     information audits 45–7

information management policy and
     strategy documents 43–5
     knowledge repositories 28–39
     naming conventions 47–9
     Orna, Elizabeth 26–7, 43
     policies 41–51
     policy documents 43–51
     retention schedules 49–50
     Webb, Jela 27
group work, introducing KIM in
     organizations 23–4

handover interviews, legacy knowledge 101
hard data repositories 30–3
Hawley Report, governance 5, 26
history
     IM 5–6
     KIM 3–6
     KM 3–5
     oral history projects, legacy knowledge
          103–4
how not to introduce KIM, case study 22
human resources, need for KIM 16

indexing, learning from failure, case study 97
information asset registers, governance 50–1
information audits, governance 45–7
information management (IM)
     advice 41
     history 5–6
information management policy and strategy
     documents, governance 43–5
information repositories *see* knowledge
     repositories
internal services teams, introducing KIM in
     organizations 20–1
interrogating unstructured data, AI
     application 110
intranets, knowledge repositories 37–9
introducing KIM in organizations 11–24
     consulting users 20
     diversity 19
     existing communities 19
     experience 23
     group work 23–24
     how not to introduce KIM 22
     internal services teams 20–1
     introduction methods 17–21
     learning and development 21
     learning from the past 21
     making the case for KIM 21–4
     organizational culture 11–24
     policies into practice 20

problem solving approach 19–22
  scenarios 21–4
  starting small 20
  synthesised approach 7

know-how pages
  case study 89
  knowledge storage 88–90
  law firms 88–90
knowledge and information management
      (KIM), definition 1–2
knowledge audits, legacy knowledge 101–3
knowledge bases, knowledge storage 86–8
knowledge capture from departing staff,
      legacy knowledge 100–6
knowledge continuity, legacy knowledge 91–2
knowledge legacy see legacy knowledge
knowledge management (KM), history 3–5
knowledge maps, knowledge storage 84–6
knowledge organizing systems 78–82
  taxonomies 78–82
knowledge projects, user engagement 87–8
knowledge repositories 28–39, 75–7
  see also knowledge storage
  approaches 90
  case studies 31, 36
  chat 37
  communication 30–3
  core organizational data 31
  data management 30–3
  e-mail 35–7
  governance 28–39
  hard data repositories 30–3
  intranets 37–9
  micro-services approach 30–3
  self-service systems 39
  semi–structured repositories 28
  SharePoint 34
  soft data repositories 33–9
  structured repositories 28
  taxonomies 81–2
  types of knowledge storage 82–90
  types of repository 30–9, 80–1
  unstructured repositories 28–30
  user consultation 77
knowledge storage
  see also knowledge repositories
  enquiries databases 82–3
  know-how pages 88–90
  knowledge bases 86–8
  knowledge maps 84–6
  types 82–90
  white pages 84–6

wikis 83–4
knowledge-sharing 53–73
  see also communities of practice; legacy
      knowledge
  approaches 72–3
  benefits 54–5
  case study 79–80
  champions model/network 66–8
  communication 56–68
  communities of interest 65
  communities of practice 53–4, 61–5, 68–72
  communities of purpose 66
  discussion forums 57–60
  online communities 61–4
  supporting successful communities 68–72
  tangible outputs 54–5
  workplace communication 56–68

law firms, know-how pages 88–90
learning and development, introducing KIM
      in organizations 21
learning from failure
  indexing 97
  legacy knowledge, case study 97
learning from the past, introducing KIM in
      organizations 21
legacy knowledge 91–106
  see also knowledge-sharing
  after-action reviews 95–100
  approaches 95–106
  archiving 104–6
  Capstone approach 104–5
  case study 97
  exit interviews 101
  handover interviews 101
  knowledge audits 101–3
  knowledge capture from departing staff
      100–6
  knowledge continuity 91–2
  learning from failure 97
  lessons learned 95–100
  oral history projects 103–4
  show and tell 93–5
  storytelling 93–5
  Volvo 99
legacy technology 8
legislation
  freedom of information legislation 6
  General Data Protection Regulation
      (GDPR) 6
lessons learned, legacy knowledge 95–100

machine learning, AI application 108–111

making KIM noticed, case study 18
making the case for KIM 21–4
management theories, organizational culture 12–13
micro-services approach, knowledge repositories 30–3

naming conventions, governance 47–9
need for KIM 15–17
 diversity 16
 human resources 16
 procurement 15
 technical capability 16–17

online communities
 approaches 72–3
 case study 62–3
 knowledge-sharing 61–4
oral history projects, legacy knowledge 103–4
organizational culture
 expert advisers 14
 introducing KIM in organizations 11–24
 and KIM 11–24
 management theories 12–13
 technology organizations 14–15
 Wenger, E. 13
organizational structures 8
Orna, Elizabeth, governance 26–7, 43

paradox, KIM 12
personalised interfaces, AI application 110
policies, governance 41–51
policies into practice, introducing KIM in organizations 20
problem solving approach, introducing KIM in organizations 19–22
procurement, need for KIM 15

questions, KIM 13–14

reification in KM 75–6
repositories see knowledge repositories
retention schedules, governance 49–50
roles
 information professionals 1
 KIM 7–8

scenarios, introducing KIM in organizations 21–4
self-service systems, knowledge repositories 39
semi-structured repositories 28
SharePoint 34, 59

case study 79–80
show and tell, legacy knowledge 93–5
soft data repositories 33–9
starting small, introducing KIM in organizations 20
storage see knowledge repositories; knowledge storage
storytelling, legacy knowledge 93–5
strategy, information management policy and strategy documents, governance 43–5
structured repositories 28
synthesised approach
 introducing KIM in organizations 7
 KIM 7

talk.gateway, discussion forum 58
taxonomies
 approaches 78–81
 case study 79–80
 classification 78–81
 knowledge organizing systems 78–82
 knowledge repositories 81–2
 types of repository 80–1
technical capability, need for KIM 16–17
technology
 see also artificial intelligence (AI)
 legacy technology 8
technology organizations, organizational culture 14–15

unstructured repositories 28–30
user consultation, knowledge repositories 77
user engagement, knowledge projects 87–8
users' language, case study 79–80

Volvo, legacy knowledge 99

Webb, Jela, governance 27
Wenger, E.
 communities of practice 61–4
 organizational culture 13
white pages, knowledge storage 84–6
wikis, knowledge storage 83–4
Wilson, T. D., communities of practice 54
workplace communication, knowledge-sharing 56–68